African American Islam

African American Islam

Aminah Beverly McCloud

Routledge
New York and London

Published in 1995 by

Routledge
29 West 35th Street
New York, NY 10001

Published in Great Britain by

Routledge
11 New Fetter Lane
London EC4P 4EE

Printed in the United States of America on acid-free paper

Library of Congress Cataloging-in-Publication Data

McCloud, Aminah Beverly
African American Islam / by Aminah Beverly McCloud
p. cm.
Includes bibliographical references and index.
ISBN 0-415-90785-3 – ISBN 0-415-90786-1 (pbk.)
1. Islam – United States. 2. Afro-Americans – Religion. I. Title.
BP67.U6M33 1995
297' .089'96073 – dc20 95-18313
CIP

Book Design and Calligraphy by Thomas Zummer

Contents

Acknowledgments

I would like to thank my husband Frederick Thaufeer Aldeen who tirelessly read, typed drafts, kept my files in order, and comforted me throughout the processes of this text. I give my sincere thanks to my children Laila and Hasim who, although completely bored with this project, helped with coffee and housework. To my oldest daughter Sadikia who telephoned occasionally to ask if I had finished yet: yes, I finished.

I also sincerely thank the many Muslim women and men who generously answered the same questions repeatedly without screaming. Special thanks to James Morris, C. Eric Lincoln, Lawrence Mamiya, Fareed Numan, Muhammad al-Ahari, and Ameenah Bey for reading, providing information, support, and editing. I also humbly acknowledge the spirits of my mother and father in keeping me on task.

Finally, thanks to the wonderful staff at Routledge – Max Zutty, Marlie Wasserman, and Adam Bohannon for their attention and dedication to this project. Special thanks goes to my blues-loving copy editor, Jay Ciaffa. I hope we do it again some time.

Introduction

THIS TEXT IS an introduction to some of the diverse community histories, beliefs, and practices that comprise African American Islam. The African American Islamic population consists of from 1.5 to 4.5 million persons distributed across at least seventeen distinct communities, and comprises the single largest ethnic group amongst Muslims in America. The presence of Islam amongst African Americans can be traced to the earliest days of their forcible exportation to this continent. Although Western literature has encouraged the notion that most African slaves practiced traditional African religions and were first introduced to monotheism via Christianity, the areas in West Africa that were raped for slaves were in fact predominantly Muslim, and had been so for six to seven hundred years prior to the slave trade. Hence, contrary to orthodox belief, a large portion of the Africans brought to this country as slaves were Muslims, and this fact is becoming increasingly clear through the discovery, translation, and interpretation of Arabic slave narratives.

The story of African American Islam is both complex and evolving, in order to provide the groundwork for a coherent account of this story, it is necessary to begin with some historical, terminological, and thematic remarks concerning both Islam in general and African American Islam in particular.

For readers who lack important background in Islam, it is necessary to begin with some basic remarks about this major world religion. At the most general level, Islam may be defined as the ongoing act of submitting one's individual will to the Will of Allah, the sole God and Creator of all worlds. Although one finds considerable diversity in Islamic expressions amongst different communities worldwide, for introductory purposes we can highlight certain core beliefs and practices as definitive features of the Islamic worldview.

The Islamic worldview centers on what Muslims consider the last revelation from Allah to humankind—the *Qur'an*, which means the "recitation." The bearer of this recitation was Muhammad ibn 'Abdullah, a seventh-century Arab, who is regarded as the last of Allah's prophets. In Islamic literature, the letters "PBUH" always follow the Prophet Muhammad's name, meaning "May the peace of blessings of Allah be upon him." First and foremost is acknowledgment that "there is no God but Allah and Muhammad is his Messenger." A Muslim is one who struggles to submit his/her will to the Will of Allah, which is spelled out in *Qur'an*ic narratives of historical recountings of incidents in past eras, and details of the guidance provided to the Prophet Muhammad in his efforts to deliver the recitation.

Islam demands that Muslims gain discipline in their struggle through a series of core practices. This set of practices includes: (1) the *shahada* or initial acknowledgment of the deity as noted above; (2) *salat* ("formal worship"), wherein believers pray and seek guidance five times daily, while engaging continuously in *Qur'an*ic recitation; (3) *sawm*, a fast wherein believers refrain from food, drink, idle talk and behavior and worldly pleasures from sunrise to sunset for thirty days the month of Ramadan; (4) *zakat*, a constant awareness of what is accumulated during the year so that the excess is taxed and shared with the community at a rate of 2.5 percent at the end of the month of Ramadan; and (5) the *hajj*, a pilgrimage to Mecca, in order to reenact the major events described in the *Qur'an* that predate and sustain the first Muslim community.

Each of these acts contributes to the discipline necessary for the submission of the Muslim's will, and together they combine to effect a worldview that has Allah's Will at its center. A portion of Allah's Will focuses on personal behavior with regard to one's self, other Muslims, and non-Muslims, such as prohibitions on the ingestion of pork and alcohol, fornication and adultery, and immodest dress and behavior. For Muslims, this social discipline and etiquette is known as *adab*. A much larger focus is given to the establishment of justice in the world. This is elaborated in terms of upholding the right and forbidding the wrong. Right and wrong are often explained by the incidents of what went on in communities before the community of the Prophet Muhammad. For example, communities that permitted greed, avarice, corruption, and sexual license were destroyed as punishment for their turning away from divine guidance.

Becoming Muslim in America thus involves stepping into a worldview that is some fourteen hundred years old. This worldview, which Muslims call *deen*, provides the framework within which all Muslims must attempt to live. It also demarcates the boundary between the world of Islam and what is known as *dunya* or *Darul Harb*, i.e., the world outside Islam.

Entry into the world of Islam also requires the beginning of a life-long study of Islamic history and Muslim scholarship, in addition to study of the *Qur'an* and the Arabic language. Most "new" Muslims enroll in community or university Arabic-language courses as soon as possible, and begin the process of collecting whatever texts on Islam that are available in their cities. The procurement and incorporation of such knowledge into daily living is augmented by contact with Muslims from all over the world.

Like all Islamic expressions, African American Islam proceeds within the general framework of practices and beliefs outlined above, and in the course of this text I will have occasion to elaborate on various aspects of the Islamic worldview as they are expressed in African American communities. In order to adequately understand African American Islamic expressions, however, it is necessary to introduce two additional notions, which pertain to the conception and constitution of community life. These are the notions of *'asabiya* and *ummah. 'Asabiya* is an Arabic concept that was ardently asserted by Ibn Khaldun, an Arab social historian of the thirteenth century. As used by Khaldun, *'asabiya* refers to kinship relations, which exert themselves in a feeling of tribal solidarity, common ethical understandings and, ultimately, in a community identity. Though Khaldun generally restricts the concept to kinship relations, I believe that the term can be usefully extended to encompass group affiliations that are somewhat broader in character, affiliations that comprise national and cultural identities. In this broader usage, *'asabiya* designates a key theme in the history of African American Islam—namely, the theme of *nation-building.* As we will see throughout this work, in one important sense, African American Islam can be viewed as the history of a people attempting to create *'asabiya* in a hostile environment.

Like *'asabiya, ummah* is a concept that refers to group affiliations and, in general Arabic usage, the term has been employed to designate a community, a nation, and/or a generation. In *Qur'an*ic usage, however, the term has a somewhat more precise meaning, referring to the "community of believers" who struggle in unison to submit their will to the Will of Allah. In this sense, the ummah is composed of many particular groups who can put aside their individual identities and mutual suspicions in order to uphold what is right, forbid injustice, and worship Allah in congregation. Ummah is thus a more general concept than *'asabiya*, unifying Muslims across specific national, ethnic, and cultural boundaries.

In contemporary Islamic discourse, this idea of *ummah* has been cast as something that is basically opposed to *'asabiya*, such that a person or community must decide whether to make its priority the formation of *'asabiya* or the experience of *ummah.* Understanding the tension between these two key concepts is crucial to understanding the nature and development of African

American Islam in this century. African American Islamic communities can be understood and differentiated largely by whether they grant priority to nation-building, on the one hand, or to experience of the ummah and participation in the world Islamic community, on the other. As we will see in the course of this work, in the first half of the twentieth century most African American Islamic communities focus on *'asabiya*, operating on the premise that the primary need for African Americans is development of a historically grounded national identity outside the confines of mainstream American society. In the second half of the century, however, this focus on *'asabiya* is branded as heretical by many Muslims both at home and abroad, and we find that many African American Islamic communities begin to prioritize the *ummah.* Unfortunately, this desire to avoid alleged heresy has often translated *to* an inability to effectively focus attention and resources on problems in African American communities across the country.

The interplay and tension between *ummah* and *'asabiya* is played out in the growth and development of individual Muslims as well as Muslim communities, and nowhere is this tension more dramatically lived out than in the life of Malcolm X/El-Hajj Malik El Shabazz. In his life, we see the potential problems if either social reality is pursued to the exclusion of the other. Malcolm X saw the dilemma presented by the tension between *'asabiya* and *ummah*, and his initial attempt to resolve this dilemma hinged on the formation of two organizations—Muslim Mosque Incorporated, dedicated to sustaining the notion of *ummah*, and the Organization of African American Unity, devoted to the pursuit of *'asabiya.* Because of his incredible insight very early in the history of African American Islam concerning the need to reconcile the requirements of *'asabiya* with those of *ummah*, Malcolm X stands as a bridge and a transition between the early and contemporary African American Muslim communities. The significance of Malcolm X will be more carefully elaborated in the section devoted to his life at the end of chapter 1.

ABOUT THIS TEXT: RESEARCH AND ORGANIZATION

This story is constructed from a variety of research materials. My primary sources have been the few scholarly texts written on African American Islam, numerous interviews with members of different communities, and reviews of various community publications (predominantly, community newspapers and newsletters). The total amount of information collected on each community could not be integrated into a single volume, so I have employed this material selectively, striving to provide an accurate picture of each community from its own point of view, with corroboration from the outside with respect to major events. While my research indicated that there are at least seventeen contemporary African American Islamic communities, the story of some communities could not be told because of scarcity of information.

In assembling my accounts of the various communities, I found myself constantly revising my own personal views with respect to the representation of Islam. I had to learn to listen carefully and not discredit information provided by interviewees in accordance with my own biases and preconceived ideas. I resolved to tell the stories of each community as best I could, and resist as much as possible any attempt to interpret beliefs and practices in summary judgments. In the course of research, I also had to come to terms with information regarded as confidential by interviewees. This was an especially difficult dilemma: as a Muslim, I hesitate to tell everything because I am aware that I might inadvertently cast a community in a light that causes it harm. But as a scholar, I am compelled to instruct and to tell the stories of each community as completely as possible. I therefore had to balance my desire to provide information with the interests and, indeed, the safety of the communities I was exploring.

In the course of my research, I discovered that most communities are islands unto themselves, which have specific criteria of loyalty to the philosophy of the group. Outsiders immediately draw suspicion, which prevails until some level of trust is established. In some communities—notably in the Nation of Islam—it was extremely difficult to gain access to the leadership. I was surprised to learn that, because I am a Muslim, many communities were even more suspicious than usual about my motivations. In these circumstances, I had to rely on the community's publications, and on interviews with members who were willing to talk. In other cases, leaders were not only accessible, but anxious to have accurate information written about their communities. Needless to say, this made my job much easier.

I begin the main body of the text with two chapters that are basically historical, devoted to describing first the early communities (1900–1960) and then the contemporary communities (1960–present). In general, this division is marked by the aforementioned shift in emphasis from the early focus on *'asabiya* to the contemporary focus on *ummah*, a shift which is facilitated in part by a sharp increase in the production and availability of Islamic literature around 1960. Of the eleven African American Islamic communities organized in the early period, I fully explore four of the five that have publications. The fifth community—the Fahammi Temples of Islam and Cultures—is not examined because interviews were not completed. In the contemporary period, seventeen communities are identified and eleven are explored. Of the seventeen contemporary communities, three are found in the early period, and the rest are either offshoots of early communities or offshoots of Muslim world communities.

Chapter 3 is an overview of contemporary African American Muslim life in its diversity. This chapter provides information on family structure, various communal adaptations of the Islamic worldview in America, and various challenges to Muslim family life. Chapter 4 examines important social issues and concerns of African American Islamic communities with regard to the broader aspects of living in the United States. Political, educational, economic, and legal challenges are all explored. Chapter 5 is an introduction to the lives of African American Muslim women, a topic of considerable interest and controversy in contemporary scholarship. In this chapter, I have relied primarily on interviews, endeavoring to allow Muslim women to articulate first-hand their own interests and concerns. Finally, in the conclusion, I provide a brief summary and offer some consolidating observations.

The Early Communities 1900 to 1960

فَلَآ أُقْسِمُ بِالشَّفَقِ ﴿١٦﴾
وَالَّيْلِ وَمَا وَسَقَ ﴿١٧﴾
وَالْقَمَرِ إِذَا اتَّسَقَ ﴿١٨﴾
لَتَرْكَبُنَّ طَبَقًا عَن طَبَقٍ ﴿١٩﴾

Behold! I call to witness the twilight of sunset, And the night and (all) that it envelops, And the moon when it becomes full, That you will invariably pass from stage to stage.

—Sura Inshiqaq 84:16–19.

In the first decades of the twentieth century, African Americans began to actively form communities that defined themselves as Islamic. Four sets of factors can be identified as the primary influences that set the stage for the implantation of Islam within African American communities: the social and political climate of America with regard to its citizens of African descent, the social and political climate in African America, Islamic retentions passed to generations through storytelling and naming, and Muslim immigration. While each of these factors plays an important role individually in the initial ideology of African American Islamic expressions, they are a collective set of influences that together are formative and cannot be separated.

The dawn of twentieth-century America saw the land in a complex web of social relations between its black and white citizens.

Blacks no longer had the protection of the federal government against discrimination and were forced to accept "separate but equal" accommodations in education, hospitals, public toilets, restaurants, and so on. There were 1,831 reported lynchings of blacks between 1891 and 1911, with estimates as high as 2,500. Major riots erupted in northern states as blacks migrated from southern states and were perceived as "new job competition" by recent European immigrants. African Americans articulated diverse responses to this precarious social and political situation. All these responses sought to recognize the integrity of black people while coping with survival. Some advocated attempts at integration into mainstream American life, in spite of the possibilities of death, while others either sought advantages within the already imposed system of segregation or complete separation by a return to Africa. Islamic responses included the quest for separate community identities within the United States, along with attempts to develop spiritual ties to the broader Islamic world community.

Early Communities: 1900–1960

Moorish Science Temple	1913
Ahmadiyyah Movement in Islam	1921
Universal Islamic Society	1926
First Muslim Mosque of Pittsburgh	1928
Islamic Brotherhood	1929
Nation of Islam	1930
Addeynu Allahe Universal Arabic Association	1930s
African American Mosque	1933
Islamic Mission Society	1939
State Street Mosque	1929
Fahamme Temple of Islam and Culture	1930s

THE MOORISH SCIENCE TEMPLE

Noble Drew Ali established the Canaanite Temple in 1913 in Newark, New Jersey, with the help of one Dr. Suliman. There were immediate challenges to Noble Drew Ali's leadership from within the Moorish community, and by 1916 internal disagreements caused a division of the Moorish-American nation into two groups. One group stated in Newark, changing its name to the Holy Moabite Temple of the World ("Moabites" being a reference to the ancient name for Moroccans). Noble Drew Ali and his followers moved to Chicago in 1925 and established the Moorish Holy Temple of Science. In 1928, this name was changed to the Moorish Science Temple of America. By this time, Ali had also established temples in Charleston, West Virginia; Milwaukee, Wisconsin; Lansing and Detroit, Michigan; Philadelphia and Pittsburgh, Pennsylvania; Pine Bluff, Arkansas; Newark, New Jersey; Cleveland and Youngstown, Ohio; Richmond and Petersburg, Virginia; and Baltimore, Maryland.[1] To give some organizational structure to this growing system of communities, Ali set up the Moorish Divine and National Movement of North America, Inc., which served as an umbrella organization for fifteen temples.

The members of Ali's movement made a nationalistic response to America's racism and to the sense of confusion that enveloped them after the end of slavery and the beginning of the migration of blacks from the southern states to the north. During this time, the escalation of hostilities resulting in lynchings and mutilation of large numbers of African Americans created an environment of fear. This fear necessitated community building, and the Moorish Science Temple of America provided a means of survival for African Americans. Thus, less than fifty years after the legal end of slavery, members of Ali's movement came together to form an Islamic community based on an assertion of nationalism that rejected integration and asserted a distinctive nationality.[2] Although Ali asserted in his newspaper that Islam was the original religion of the so-called Negro, he did not say how he knew this information.[3] Perhaps there were retentions of Islamic practice in the black environment that were constantly given life in stories passed on in families.[4]

Islamic belief in the Moorish community focused on central *Qur'an*ic concepts such as justice, a purposeful creation of mankind, freedom of will, and humankind as the generator of personal action (both good and bad). *Qur'an*ic principles concerning the nature of reality as spiritual and the nature of human existence as co-eternal with the existence of time also figured prominently. At the core of Moorish teachings was the assertion that the primary need of African Americans in the first decades of the twentieth century was a historically accurate nationality—i.e., a national identity that gave them some connection with a homeland.[5] Community members were taught to identify themselves as Moorish, and were asked not to use designations such as Negro, Ethiopian, or Colored. More overtly political stances were also taken within the community—for example, members were asked to refuse to serve in the military.[6]

Noble Drew Ali also was clear on what constitutes Islam. To the question "What is Islam?" he responded:

> Islam is a very simple faith. It requires man to recognize his duty toward God (Allah) his Creator, his fellow creatures, it teaches the supreme duty of living at peace with one's surroundings. . . . The name means Peace. The goal of a man's life according to Islam is peace with everything. . . . The cardinal doctrine of Islam is unity of the Father (Allah), We believe in One God. Allah is all God, all mercy, and all power, he is perfect and holy, all wisdom, all knowledge, all truth. . . . He is free from all defects, holy, transcendent. He is personal to us in so far as we can see His attributes working for us and in us but He is nevertheless impersonal, He is infinite, perfect and holy. . . . nor do we believe that God is a helpless, inactive, inert force. . . .

> Nothing happens without his knowledge and will. He neither begets nor is He begotten because these are traits of frail and weak humanity. This unity of Allah is the first and foremost pillar of Islam and every other belief hangs upon it.[7]

There is no evidence that the Moorish Science Temple of America had access to even most of the basic Islamic texts, with the possible exception of the *Qur'an.*[8] It is well known that the literacy rate in America at the turn of this century was very low for all ethnicities. This reality would have necessarily affected African Americans, although some probably could read, and could with assistance or direction come to some level of understanding of the English translation of the *Qur'an.* Attaining literacy and becoming informed about subjects such as African history, world geography, and mathematics thus became a fundamental goal of the Moorish community as well as other African American communities. Toward this end, the Moorish Science Temple published a substantial amount of literature in the African American community.[9]

Noble Drew Ali published a particular "scripture" for his community entitled the *Holy Koran of the Moorish Science Temple* (first published in 1927). It was a pamphlet produced for members of the community by members of the community. This text, also called the *Circle Seven,* was designed to help members build knowledge of themselves as Moorish Muslims.

In this text, Ali asserted that the purpose of the Moorish Science Temple was "the uplifting of fallen humanity." He also asserted that

> the lessons of this pamphlet are not for sale, but for the sake of humanity. As I am a prophet and the servant is worthy of his hire, you can receive this pamphlet at expense. The reason these lessons have not been known is because the Moslems of India, Egypt

> and Palestine had these secrets and kept them back from the outside world, and when the time came appointed by Allah they loosened the keys and free these secrets, and for the first time in ages have these secrets been delivered in the hands of the Moslems of America.[10]

The name of the religion, Ali declared, was "Islamism." The guiding principles of nationhood were to be symbolized in the flag—a red flag with a five-pointed green star in the center with the respective points standing for love, truth, peace, freedom, and justice. The holy day was Friday, because "Friday is the day on which man was formed in flesh, and it was on Friday when he departed out of flesh."

The Moorish Science community believed that most, if not all African Americans had a religious heritage that was lost as a consequence of slavery. A concrete alternative that was not completely unknown among the Africans was a return to the religion of their ancestors, particularly those in Morocco—Islam. Noble Drew Ali had some knowledge or contact with Moroccans or had read some history of ancient families, enabling him to make connections between Canaanites, Moabites, and Moors. As Wilson points out, however, there is still considerable unclarity about the source of many of Ali's key ideas:

> Scholars have been able to trace the sources for most of Noble Drew Ali's scripture, the *Circle Seven Koran*, but no one seems to have discovered the source of his ideas about Moorish Science itself, or the Moorish Empire.[11]

Ali taught his community that the Moors introduced Islam to the New World and that the Moors' home was Morocco. He also taught that a person must have a nationality before they could have a God. Members of Ali's community changed the surnames given to them by slave holders to El or Bey, as they were taught that these surnames were the most common in Morocco and signified their connection to a nation. Morocco became Mecca. Stories of contact with Moroccans, travels to Morocco, and a warm welcome from the Moroccan people further concretized and affirmed this choice.

Rejecting the European-American designation "Negro" as both derogatory and meaningless, members of Ali's community filled in "Moor" on federal, state, and city forms requiring the identification of ethnicity.[12] Members of the community were not taught formal prayers (*salat*), fasting during the month of Ramadan (*sawm*), or about pilgrimage to Mecca (*hajj*). Rather, they were taught about community spirit, how to establish organized conventions, how to conduct Friday meetings, and how to pay "dues."[13] Members were taught to pray three times daily facing east.[14] Evidence suggests that they were unaware of the concepts of *zakat* (a 2.5 percent tax on excess wealth) and *tauheed* (the concept of the oneness of Allah). Although members realized that Muhammad was *the* Prophet and the *Qur'an* the message, they still had their own book and their own prophet.[15] The latter point is amply evident in the Moorish-American Prayer, which says:

> ALLAH the Father of the Universe, the Father of Love, Truth, Peace, Freedom and Justice. ALLAH is my Protector, my Guide, and my Salvation by night and by day, through His Holy Prophet, DREW ALI. (Amen)[16]

As far as we know, the men and women in this community did not have access to *hadith* literature (narrative accounts of the sayings and actions of Prophet Muhammad) or any other Islamic literature, except that which was in public libraries or in bookstores at the turn of the century. Nevertheless, men and women put into effect the Islamic norms of hospitality, modesty, and gender separateness. Men were encouraged to work in any legal vocation, and most found work in even the most highly segregated industries in the North. Outside of work, the men donned the Moroccan fez and wore either African robes or Western attire. Women wore a turban seven yards long and three inches wide of wrapped material (usually red, although it could be any color).

Men and women received their everyday guidance also from the *Holy Koran of the Moorish Science Temple.* Men followed chapter 20, "Holy Instruction and Warnings for All Young Men":

> 1. Beware, young man, beware of all the allurements of wantonness, and let not the harlot tempt thee to excess in her delights.

and chapter 22, "Duty of a Husband":

> 1. Take unto thyself a wife and obey the ordinance of Allah; take unto thyself a wife, and become a faithful member of society. . . .
> 5. O cherish her as a blessing sent to thee from Heaven. . . .
> 9. Trust thy secrets in her breast; her counsels are sincere, thou shalt not be deceived.

While there are no holy instructions on the duty of women, there are "Marriage Instructions for Man and Wife from The Noble Prophet" in chapter 21:

> 3. Remember thou art made man's reasonable companion, not the slave of his passion; the end of thy being is not merely to gratify his

> loose desire, but to assist him in the toils of life, to soothe his heart with thy tenderness and recompense his care with soft endearments.

Regardless of whether they were literate, members who could afford to do so acquired a Maulana Muhammed Ali translation of the *Holy Qur'an* when it became available in the United States. Later, when copies of the Yusef Ali translation of the *Holy Qur'an* became available, members of the community generally also acquired copies of it.[17] In addition to these texts, there were several newspapers that emerged in the Moorish-American community: the *Moorish Guide National,* first published as a weekly on Fridays in 1928, and the *Moorish Science Monitor.*[18] By the 1950s, members of the Temple were also publishing the *Moorish Review* out of Richmond, Virginia. It is important to note that the teachings found in the Temple's publications are nonspecific; they give only very general guidance for living. It should also be noted that these teachings have never changed.

In addition to broad religious instruction, the Temple's papers also encouraged economic diligence and independence. This goal was pursued in part via the Moorish Manufacturing Corporation, which manufactured products such as Moorish Mineral and Heating Oil, and Moorish Bath Compound and Tonic. In the *Moorish Guide National* of August 1928, a caption promoting these products reads: "Our men, women and children should be taught to believe in the capacity of our group to succeed in business in spite of the trials and failures of some of them."

It has been estimated that ten thousand African Americans passed through one of the at least fifteen Moorish Science Temples by 1950. The community in general has been very active in feeding the poor, providing drug and alcohol rehabilitation, and creating wholesome, disciplined community life. Pearl Ali, the first wife of Noble Drew Ali, has been especially devoted to these social concerns, having established and led the Young People's Moorish

League, which was very active in city neighborhoods. As of this writing, she is still living in Chicago.

Noble Drew Ali was murdered in 1920, and buried in Burr Oak Cemetery in Chicago. The circumstances surrounding his death remain shrouded in mystery. The *Chicago Defender* reports his death and some of the circumstances surrounding it in a story of 20 July 1920. The story begins with a reference to the murder of Claude D. Greene, Ali's business manager, by other members of the Moorish community. At the time of this murder, the police moved in and arrested a number of community members, including Noble Drew Ali himself. Ali died soon after his release on bail, either from the complications of police beatings, or from a beating administered by community rivals. However he died, it was understood within the community that he would reincarnate.

Ali did not name a successor, and two main contenders immediately vied for leadership—C. Kirkman Bey (Ali's former secretary), and John Givens-El (Ali's former chauffeur). At the Unity Convention held in 1929, the council of governors of the community elected C. Kirkman Bey to the highest office of Grand Sheik. During the convention, however, John Givens-El declared that he was the reincarnation of Noble Drew Ali, and this led to division within the general community. As Wilson reports, "Some say that at this time there were twenty-one Moorish Science temple branch temples; others say fifteen, of which eight followed Kirkman Bey, and seven followed Givens-El."[19]

THE AHMADIYYAH MOVEMENT IN ISLAM

Almost at the same time that Noble Drew Ali was establishing the Moorish Science Temple, other African American Islamic communities were beginning to form. One such movement was the Ahmadiyyah Movement in Islam, which originated in India.[20] In the first half of the twentieth century, many African American Muslim communities were influenced by the mission of Indian Ahmadis to the United States. The missionaries set up a series of mosques on the east coast and in the midwest, all of which were identified by the preface "the First Mosque." Missionaries were organized to set up study groups focusing on the beliefs of Islam and the fundamentals of Islamic practice. Meeting several times weekly, interested people were taught Arabic and *Qur'an*ic studies.

The Ahmadi community published the first English-language Muslim newspaper in the United States—the *Moslem Sunrise*—in 1921. It also founded the journal *Review of Religions.* African Americans in this community held limited positions of leadership, prestige, and learning. They published the first English *Qur'an* for general use in America in 1917. This community used Bukhari and Muslim *hadith* literature, but held that the guiding principle is to accept all *hadith* except those which run contrary to the *Qur'an.*[21] Their prolific production of texts and newsletters were valuable assets for the promotion of Islam. The Ahmadi provided a majority of the literature available to all African American Muslim communities for many decades, especially *Qur'an*s and commentary on the *Qur'an.*

The first "missionaries" taught that God is active in this world, determining and designing the course of events in special ways.[22] Death is not the end of existence for human beings; there is a day of judgment and a hereafter. Heaven or Hell are places whose inhabitants are determined, selected, or assigned by their deeds on earth. Ahmadi emphasis on a living relationship with God and their belief that revelatory experience is still possible opened up the way for more contemporary prophets. Missionaries asserted that "when evil runs rampant in this world, God chooses from among His most devoted servants, selects one and speaks, revealing his purpose and charging those servants with the duty to guide the world."[23] "Missionaries" also introduced systematic Islamic study that had no reference to nationalism.

Graduates (male and female) of these courses, which spanned several years, were given the title *shaykh.* One-time members of this community asserted in interviews that by the early 1930s there were fifty *shaykhs* licensed to teach Islam around the country (the number of women was estimated at half). Missionaries cultivated quite a few of their followers from members of the Moorish Science Temple who were apparently displeased with the limitations of the teachings on nationalism.

African American Muslims in this community were inheritors of the theology and philosophy of the Ahmadiyyah movement on the Indian subcontinent. A central portion of this philosophy, which expanded the notion of prophethood beyond the Prophet Muhammad, was not new to America.[24] Another aspect of the philosophy that may have more bearing here is the notion of accommodation to those in authority. The Ahmadi self-understanding asserts that "divine messengers have belonged to different levels of spiritual greatness and have fulfilled in different degrees the divine purpose which determined their advent."[25] While asserting that the greatest messenger was the Holy Prophet, they also asserted that Hazrat Mirza Ghulam Ahmad of Qadian was the promised Messiah and Mahdi (understood as a deputy of Prophet Muhammad). Diverging from most Muslim world understandings, the Ahmadi community believed that "the institution of revelation and the coming of prophets continues after the Holy Prophet," that Jesus, both prophet and mortal, died a natural death, and that the coming Messiah is not Jesus but a follower of the Holy Prophet—namely Hazrat Mirza Ghulam Ahmad, who was to come in Jesus's likeness and spirit, as John had come in the spirit of Elias.

The membership of the Ahmadiyyah movement in America during the years 1917–1960 was predominately African American. The "mission houses" (mosque-activity centers) were headed by African Americans in African American areas of various cities. A significant number of African American jazz musicians were members of this community—Talib Daud, Art Blakey, Yusef Lateef, Ahmad Jamal, and McCoy Tyner, to name a few. These musicians were major propagators of Islam in the world of jazz even though the subject of music was often a source of debate with the subcontinent Ahmadis. Some even developed their own jargon—a unique blend of bebop and Arabic.[26] There also developed a merchant class of men in this community (comprised mainly of vendors), due to lack of opportunities for formal education. Self-employment became a way to earn a living while at the same time maintaining the freedom to propagate Islam, and to say prayers five times daily and the Jumah prayer on Friday with ease.[27]

One major community of Ahmadis was headed by Wali Akram from 1934 to 1937 in Cleveland, Ohio. He established a "ten-year plan" for a financial base for the community that involved a savings plan where money was kept in a savings and loan institution. He networked this plan to affiliated *masajid* (the preferred Arabic word for the Anglicized mosques in Akron, Youngstown, Dayton, Columbus, Ohio and in Pittsburgh, Pennsylvania). By the 1940s there were two hundred people in the masjid in Cleveland. Records were kept on every member including their birth names, name changes, addresses, and the date they became Muslim. Interethnic marriages, although not the norm, were frequent. The international character of the community lent itself to the Islamic stance against racism and social division. Families were close knit, using the masjid as the base for class and social interaction.

As the twentieth century progressed, the direct personal influence of the Ahmadi missionaries declined. Early members left the movement for a variety of reasons. Dissension arose due to the fact that African Americans were never appointed as missionaries. [28] The title of *shakyh* acknowledged their accomplishments in Islamic studies, but did not give them any authority over communities. Surviving original members of this community complained that the effects of colonialism also came with the missionaries, who insisted on Indian customs and interpretations, rather than seeing African American culture as having something to offer American Islam. Islamic study also raised questions over the Ahmadi notion of prophethood, prompting others to leave the community.

THE ISLAMIC MISSION OF AMERICA

The Islamic Mission of America, Inc. (also known as the State Street Mosque or Islamic Brotherhood) began with the efforts of

Shaykh Dauod Ahmed Faisal in New York in 1924.[29] Shaykh Dauod claimed that his efforts at spreading Islam were sanctioned, asserting that he received a letter of permission from Jordan to "legitimately" spread Islam in 1925. Along with its central masjid in New York, Faisal's organization from the beginning acted as an umbrella for many smaller Muslim communities that dotted the northeastern coastline. It has been estimated that over sixty thousand conversions to Islam took place in Shaykh Dauod's community in his lifetime.

All of the affiliated communities considered themselves aligned with other Sunni Muslims in the world; they fasted during the month of Ramadan, made five daily prayers, endeavored to make the *hajj*, and often dressed like Arabs.[30] Just as the Moorish Science Temple taught African Americans that they were not Negroes, but were originally Muslims, so did Shaykh Dauod. But after this point of commonality, the Moorish Science political stance and that of the Islamic Mission parted company. Whereas the Moorish Science Temple community resisted attempts by the United States government to draft its men into the armed forces, the Islamic Mission of America permitted its male followers to join. In Faisal's understanding enlistment was necessary to accommodate to the geographic reality of blacks here in America, even though their citizenship was questionable. Faisal thought that blacks should reclaim their Islamic heritage and also lay claim to an American allegiance.

In efforts to reclaim Islamic alliances, ties were forged with the greater Muslim world when Muslim seamen from Madagascar, Yemen, and Somalia docked in New York harbor and sought congregational prayers, personal supplies, and Muslim friendships in Shaykh Dauod's community. The numbers of sick and dying Muslim seamen prompted Shaykh Dauod to help them take out insurance policies, so that in the event of death they would have a *Salat al-Janazah* (funeral prayer), a burial, and their families notified.[31] This gesture went far in earning wide respect among Muslim immigrants and visitors for Shaykh Dauod's community.

In the various communities that affiliated themselves with the

Islamic Mission movement, teachings were taken from what the members understood as the Sunni Islamic world. The Islamic Mission movement distributed Islamic literature, using the Ahmadi translation of the *Qur'an* and, later, Yusuf Ali's translation, the *Holy Qur'an.* Additionally, like the Moorish Science Temple, the Islamic Mission of America provided its community members with identity cards (another example of the perception of the need for nationhood). Apparently, in this community the teaching priorities lay in the fundamentals of belief in Islam. The early sustained contact with immigrant and visiting Muslims is at least one reason for this focus emerging as dominant.

The communities under Shaykh Dauod embraced certain common Islamic practices such as no taking of pictures, taking shoes off when entering the house, and squatting when drinking any liquid unless already seated. These practices probably were learned from the seamen and immigrants who entered Islamic Mission communities. The inability to read, write, or speak (more than a few phrases) in Arabic limited further access to information regarding traditional Islamic doctrine. The educated as well as the illiterate depended almost totally on oral transmission of *'adab* (etiquette). Through this method certain customs concerning spatial arrangement of the home and female-male relationships began to take shape in Islamic Mission communities, and these customs have become more firmly entrenched during the latter half of the century. (These customs will be more fully discussed in later chapters.)

One source asserts that in 1930 or 1932 Shaykh Dauod bought an estate in Fisherkill (or Fishkill), New York to build a small city to be called New Medina. The community's own writings do not dispute this issue but state that:

> In the late 1940s, Mother Khadijah traveled with her husband and others upstate New York to look for land Sheikh had seen in a dream. In Duchess County, in the mountains not far from Beacon, N.Y., in an area

> called Wicoppee Hook, named after the famous Indian Chief Wicoppee, they found the land. It was a large piece of property. . . . Sheikh perceived this property being the ideal spot for the first Muslim Community in America. . . . It was called "Madinat Assalam.". . . Madinat Assalam was lost about seven years later, due to the lack of unity and maturity of the people it was for.[32]

After three years, probably due to lack of available resources, this project was abandoned and the community returned to the State Street Mosque. From this location all the normal masjid functions were held, such as weddings, funerals, and Islamic education classes.

As for his own literary contributions, in 1954 Shaykh Dauod wrote *Islam: The True Religion of Humanity*, in which he provides "lots of information" on Muslim countries.[33] Among the newsletters and journals published from the State Street Mosque was *Sahabiyat*, a magazine for Muslim women. Included in the contents were: Islamic Art/Education, Health/Science, and Homemaking. Hajja "Mother" Khadijah Faisal (Shaykh Dauod's wife) was president of the Muslim Ladies Cultural Society of the Islamic Mission of America, and was clearly an inspiration to the young women in the community. The influence of Shaykh Dauod stretches from the beginning until the present in the philosophies of communities that adhere to his teachings. (The Shaykh died in February, 1980.) Though the creation of an economic base has never been realized to any substantial degree, the Islamic Mission of America remains one of the most influential communities in African American Islam.

THE FIRST MOSQUE OF PITTSBURGH

The First Mosque of Pittsburgh came into contact with all the previously mentioned philosophies, and its development as a community reflects each encounter. This community began without a name but with a search for Islam that first led the members to adopt the philosophy and materials of Noble Drew Ali.[34] Organizing themselves around Ali's teachings and concretizing the foundation of the community led to a membership of over one thousand by 1934. The fundamental notion in Islam of the oneness of Allah and the principles of love, truth, peace, freedom, and justice carried this community for a number of years. But several years after its foundation, the main teacher of this community, Walter Smith Bey, invited Dr. Yusef Khan (an Ahmadi) to speak to the community. Dr. Khan, an Ahmadi Muslim from India, took over the education of the community, initiating another stage in growth and development. This caused a division in the community, as some wished to continue with the guidance provided by Noble Drew Ali, rather than expand their Islamic understanding under the tutelage of Dr. Khan.

Dr. Khan's teachings and activities included:

1. Use of the Qur'an as the primary source of religious information.
2. Use of *hadith* of the Prophet Muhammad as the secondary source of spiritual guidance.
3. Encouraging members to accept Muslim names.
4. Establishing a school.
5. Performance of Islamic weddings.
6. Teaching the five daily prayers.

As part of Dr. Khan's educational system, classes were taught four times weekly: twice on Sunday, and once each on Wednesday and Friday.[35] This shift in learning gave Islamic understanding priority over "nationalist sentiments." The community learned their prayers and how to read the *Qur'an* in both Arabic and English. Their instruction also included the study of *hadith, dawah* (propagation of Islam), funeral preparation and prayers, and prayers for special occasions.

Leadership in this community was truly consensual. Women

were as important as men when it came to community business, and this was manifest in their active participation in educational classes and leadership. By 1934, thirteen men and women had completed the requirements of the school and were accordingly given the title of "Sheik." In addition to the level of confidence this process inspired, it gave the community a core of learned people to both spread Islam and to lead the community without reliance on one person.

During this time of growth, however, there emerged a new conflict pertaining to Dr. Khan's teachings. This conflict, which arose in 1935, centered on Dr. Khan's claim that Hazrat Mirza Ghulam Ahmad was the prophet who came after Muhammad (PBUH).

After much debate, most of the community concluded, against Dr. Khan, that there would be no "compromise on the finality of Muhammad's (PBUH) prophethood." This decision caused not only a second division in the community, but also the need for a division of property and assets.

Despite this conflict the community remained intact, guided by the twin goals of securing a charter and obtaining ownership of a building, and by the fundamentals of Islam given in the classes by Dr. Khan. It took ten years of saving and fund-raising, but on 26 February 1945 both goals were realized when this community finally became the First Muslim Mosque of Pittsburgh, Pennsylvania. Continuing with its precedent-setting inclusion of women in governance, the community set forth a constitution, of which Mrs. Hakim's text prints a portion of article 2:

> The purpose of the First Muslim Mosque is to disseminate the true principles of the Religion of Al-Islam, to build and maintain Mosques, to cultivate friendship of other people, to establish the Jumah Prayer among its members, to furnish aid in case of sickness, death, or permanent disability, to endeavor to unite with other

> Muslim units in the United States and by legal and proper means to elevate the moral, intellectual, social, and spiritual condition of all members.[36]

Muslim women demonstrated their leadership qualities by their establishment of the Young Muslim Women's Association, for which they secured a charter on 17 May 1946. In the 1950s, these Muslim women also organized a Red Crescent Club, following the lead of African American women who had organized a club by the same name during the 1920s in Detroit, modeled on the American Red Cross. The activities of the Young Muslim Women's Association included aid to dependent children, widows, and the elderly. These efforts were replicated in subcharters in Braddock and Philadelphia, Pennsylvania; Cleveland, Ohio; Kirkwood, and St. Louis, Missouri; and Jacksonville, Florida.[37] Muslim men in the community followed this initiative, and later formed an unchartered Young Men's Muslim Association. This association performed social services in the local community, the most significant of which was an Islamic Boys' Club.

It is clear from sparse information that this community represents a dynamic spirit of Islam in the first half of the twentieth century. The grandchildren and great-grandchildren of its founders still struggle to keep this hard-won spirit alive.

THE NATION OF ISLAM

Lastly, we turn our attention to the most popular and most documented community of this early period, the Nation of Islam. The Nation of Islam, an indigenous African American Islamic expression founded by Wali Fard Muhammad and developed by Elijah Muhammad, became the American media's prototype of Islam in the African American community. The core of the philosophy of the Nation was characterized by a combination of messianism and a form of chiliasm. A fundamental belief in Allah as one with no sons or partners dominated the theology, with an ethical emphasis on man's ability to correct man. Elijah Muhammad was Allah's special messenger to "the so-called Negro." Armed with this information and firm in its belief, this community of African American Muslims set out to build a visible and viable nation. First on the agenda, as in the Moorish Science Temple, was the need to cleanse the spirit, mind, and body. Alcohol, gambling, fornication, adultery, dancing, and other similar activities ceased immediately, and abstinence was enforced by investigators. Dietary restrictions included not only prohibitions on pork, but also on other foods considered to be "fast roads to death" and reminders of slavery, such as collard greens, cornbread, and neckbones. The community's dietary habits reflected both members' circumstances and their aspirations—diet included fish, the protein and vitamins of which helped keep the mind alert and the muscles strong, teas for energy and mental alertness, rice as a staple, and so on.

These regulations on almost every aspect of life had visible results. The Nation had a characteristic dress, countenance, set of behaviors, and discipline. They did not fear repeating the teaching of Elijah Muhammad on who they were and who white people were in the scheme of creation.

> To commemorate his rebirth, the convert drops his last name and is known simply by his first name and the letter X. To facilitate identification among Muslims having the same first name and belonging to the same temple, numbers are prefixed to the X.
>
> The symbol X has a double meaning: implying "ex," it signifies that the Muslim is no longer what he was; and as "X," it signifies an unknown quality or quantity. It at once repudiates the white man's name and announces the rebirth of Black Man, endowed

> with a set of qualities the white man does not have and does not know.[38]

Selling *Final Call* newspapers, bean pies, and providing a physically different presence in the black community, members of the Nation were viewed positively, though with some suspicion. The Nation of Islam, like the Moorish Science Temple, was a direct challenge to black Christianity, but they nevertheless were not seen as a threat to the general community life. On the contrary, members of the Islamic community were applauded for their moral uprightness and cleanliness.

Not surprisingly, however, their philosophies and self-assertions caused a good deal of concern to the majority white community. Both journalists and FBI informants painted a picture of an extremely reactionary, nationalistic movement, citing "peculiarities" in the Nation's doctrine that would be viewed negatively by white America. These peculiarities include calling white people "devils" and promoting the concept that black men were really gods. The American press also considered as "radical" the notion of a separate physical place for African Americans. No one mentioned the fact that the debate on a nation for blacks had been around for at least two centuries in both the African American community and the European-American community.

Indeed, groups of whites had also called for a return of blacks to Africa as a solution to the so-called "Negro problem" in the years prior to the Civil War. Benjamin Ringer describes the sentiment of these white colonization groups (who were comprised primarily of northerners) as follows:

> Opposed to the continued enslavement of the black but at the same time convinced that the emancipated black had had no real place in white society, a number of white Northerners sought to resolve this dilemma by proposing the colonization of the black in Africa or elsewhere.

> To accomplish this purpose, they established the American Colonization Society in 1817.[39]

While many blacks were sympathetic to the appeal of this project, very few actually emigrated. In the decades prior to the start of the twentieth century, the attitude on the part of whites that "the blacks had to go elsewhere and establish themselves as a people"[40] and the black determination to have a say in how that establishment would occur led to two conspicuous nations in one place. What this also points to is that emancipation from slavery obviously did not result in blacks being included in American society. With this history, how could Elijah Muhammad's goal of a separate state be perceived? It certainly could not be perceived as unusual at the time, or for that matter now.

Within the context of this nationalist perspective, the Nation of Islam put forth an agenda called the *Muslim Program*.

> *What the Muslims Want*
>
> This is the question asked most frequently by both the whites and the Blacks. The answer to this question I shall state as simply as possible.
>
> 1. We want freedom. . . .
> 2. We want justice. Equal justice under the law. . . .
> 3. We want equality of opportunity.
> 4. We want our people in America whose parents or grandparents were descendants from slaves, to be allowed to establish a separate state or territory of their own—either on this continent or elsewhere. We believe that our former slave masters are obligated to provide such land and that the area must be

fertile and minerally rich. . . .

5. We want freedom for all Believers of Islam now held in federal prisons. . . .
6. We want an immediate end to the police brutality and mob attacks against the so-called Negro throughout the United States.
7. As long as we are not allowed to establish a state or territory of our own, we demand not only equal justice under the laws of the United States, but equal employment opportunities—NOW!
8. We want the government of the United States to exempt our people from ALL taxation as long as we are deprived of equal justice under the laws of the land.
9. We want equal education—but separate schools up to 16 for boys and 18 for girls on the condition that the girls be sent to women's colleges and universities. . . .
10. We believe that intermarriage or race mixing should be prohibited. We want the religion of Islam taught without hindrance or suppression.

Members of the Nation focused on particular portions of the *Qur'an*, examples of which included emphasis on the following:

1. The beneficence and mercy of Allah toward those who believe in him.

2. The distortions of the Bible.
3. Islam as the religion of salvation and truth.
4. The Qur'an's challenge to disbelievers to "produce a chapter like it."
5. Dietary prohibitions.
6. The dictum that forbids "compulsory conversion" and teaches that a Muslim should never be the aggressor "but fight in the way of Allah with those who fight against you."
7. Respect for women.

Since the Nation's agenda diverged somewhat from traditional Islamic doctrine, some "orthodox" Muslims accused them of illicit innovation and, indeed, heresy. To these accusations, Abdul Basit Naeem offers the following response, drawing on the words of Elijah Muhammad:

> I am, of course, fully aware of the fact that some of the teachings of Mr. Elijah Muhammad . . . would not be acceptable to Moslems in the East without, perhaps, some sort of an explanation by the author or by someone who can interpret them well. As he told me a few months ago, "My brothers in the East were never subject to conditions of slavery and systematic brainwashing by the slavemasters for as long a period of time as my people here were subjected. I cannot, therefore, blame them if they differ with me in certain interpretations of the Message of Islam."[41]

Mr. Naeem goes on to assert that differences between traditional Islam and the Nation's teachings are not as significant as some have suggested:

> As far as I am concerned, I consider the differences between Islam of the East and the teachings of Mr. Elijah Muhammad to be of relatively minor importance *at this time,* because these are not related to the SPIRIT OF ISLAM.[42]

The Honorable Elijah Muhammad recognized that *myths* are an important foundation in all human communities. Hence, myths of creation, myths of world order, myths that explain the present and the future were all seated at the core of the Nation of Islam. These myths provided a knowledge-base for members of the Nation in the form of stories concerning the "Original Man," the "colored man," and a place of origin. The levels of culture-building on which Mr. Muhammad worked simultaneously fit together like the pieces of a symphony. While providing identity in the manner of most cultures—i.e., with a name—he at once connected and disconnected each individual to slave history. An X denoted the fragility of existence in the United States for African Americans, and at the same time revealed knowledge of that fact. All cultures have divisions of labor, means of sustenance, hierarchies of knowledge, and an understanding of their place in creation. This is the matrix into which Mr. Muhammad situated his community.

Mr. Muhammad also built businesses and provided a plan for the growth of the nation. He quickly established a mosque, and then expeditiously "launched the Nation on the route to economic self-sufficiency through business enterprises."[38] These businesses ranged from farms to clothing manufacture to grocery stores. Supplying both Muslim and non-Muslim African Americans, these enterprises prospered as concrete evidence of nationhood. In the aftermath of a depression, there were finally jobs and professions for African Americans—managers, tailors, secretaries, accountants, and so on. His blueprint for his nation was to take concrete form over the next forty years. The Honorable Elijah Muhammad obviously understood, along with Noble Drew Ali, that a "people" need all those things that define societies in the world.

During the 1920s the emerging prominence of the Garvey movement, the Moorish Science Temple, and the Ahmadiyyah community, along with the general anti-black attitudes of white Americans, made for a chaotic religious and political environment within the African American community. Alongside the religious crises of the European community and the economic collapse of the United States, the spiritual waters were pulsing with prophetic rhetoric. Nevertheless, the fact that the Nation of Islam emerged during a period of intense labor agitation, lingering hostilities over the slavery issue, and economic panic does not lead to a conclusion that their existence was purely a result of that troubled social situation. Rather, it is possible that African Americans would have sought to reclaim their Islamic heritage had the environment been different. The drive to know oneself and one's past is especially compelling for the oppressed.

With access to the *Holy Qur'an* and its commentary produced by the Ahmadi community, along with the *Final Call* and pamphlets from the Islamic Mission Movement, the Garvey movement, and the Moorish Science Temple, African American Muslims within the Nation of Islam began the process of cultural formation. As in Muslim communities throughout history, the need to particularize what is celebrated and to prioritize some beliefs over others is seen in all these African American communities. For African Americans, the Qur'anic emphasis on social justice becomes, after tauheed, the highest priority.

In the first part of this century, the Nation of Islam certainly laid the foundation for a "true" community.[44] They had myths of origin, a sense of self, industry, moral boundaries, and spirituality. As the solidarity of this young community grew so did its resources and thus its successes in the marketplace.[45]

GROWTH AND TENSION: THE SIGNIFICANCE OF MALCOLM X

The preceding discussion has provided a glimpse of leaders who were remarkably gifted in their ability to make some sense of African American history in the absence of critical historical tools, and to then take their conclusions as visions to their community. Noble Drew Ali, Elijah Muhammad, Shaykh Dauod Faisal, and others looked at the human condition in their community, saw its history, and described a disconnection from ancestral lineage. Each viewed the African American community as a "lost nation" that needed to be reconnected to its origin, and each saw Islam as the way to achieve this reconnection. But the growth of Islam under the historical circumstances confronting African Americans led to a crucial tension that the early communities were just beginning to experience: the tension between the demands of *'asabiya* (nation-building) and commitment to the *ummah* (the world community of Islamic believers).

The tension between these two key forces, which has continued to inform the growth of Islam in America, is powerfully exemplified in the life of one of the most prominent African American Muslim leaders of the second half of this century— Malcolm X/El-Hajj Malik El-Shabazz. Malcolm's initial encounter with Islam was through the Nation of Islam, and was facilitated by a questioning of the prevailing religious views held by many African Americans, Christian views in particular.

> And where the religion of every other people on earth taught its believers of a God with whom they could identify, a God who at least looked like one of their own kind, the slave master injected his Christian religion into this "Negro." This "Negro" was taught to worship an alien god having the same blond hair, pale skin, and blue eyes as the slave master.

> This religion taught the "Negro" that black was a curse. It taught him to hate everything black, including himself. It taught that everything white was good, to be admired, respected, and loved.[46]

Upon learning a small piece of the history of humankind—that the human race had its origins in Africa, and that history had literally been "whitewashed" for centuries—Malcolm described himself as "dumbstruck." In the Nation of Islam, Malcolm found a space where an African American could be a subject, rather than an object, and could speak about reality without muting his words or compromising his manhood. Islam within the Nation provided an alternative history for slavery, a rationale for the condition of African Americans, and a method for experiencing nationhood here on earth.

Malcolm's initial encounter with Islam included intimate study of scripture as well as commitment to discipline, imposed from within and without. By and large, Malcolm's early days in the Nation are characterized by complete submission to the teachings of Elijah Muhammad, as is evidenced by his public speeches and private conversations during this period, which are prefaced with "the Honorable Elijah Muhammad teaches us. . . ." At this time, Malcolm saw himself as being in complete submission to the Will of Allah by being in submission to the will of his servant, Elijah Muhammad. In this capacity, Malcolm was of course primarily committed to the project of nation-building for African American Muslims.

In the later portion of Malcolm's life, however, his almost exclusive emphasis on nation-building is altered, as he begins to see the value of participating in the broader community of Islamic believers. Malcolm's views shifted most notably during a period of reading and discourse that included his pilgrimage to Mecca. During this time, Malcolm learned that the move into Islam is a move into a fourteen-hundred-year-old order that is both constant and inspiring, an order of which one can partake without reference to color. In this order, one finds an everyday, expanded notion of "brotherhood," which extends beyond a brotherhood developed along strictly racial or ethnic lines. The crucial question that arises at this juncture is: Can one reconcile this broader Islamic understanding with the demands of an Islam focused on African American nation-building? Though Malcolm did not see any problem in asserting Islamic brotherhood, he clearly was worried about Muslims overlooking injustice in their own communities for the sake of participation in the larger community of believers. He specifically wondered how he could give himself over to the world of Muslims when the daily injustices heaped upon African Americans had not changed. Hence, Malcolm by no means gave himself over exclusively to the *ummah*, as we can see from this exchange with a reporter on his return from the pilgrimage. When the reporter asked if he would now call himself El-Hajj Malik El-Shabazz, Malcolm responded, "Not until the condition of my people changes."

Malcolm's thought and action represent the tension between *'asabiya* and *ummah*, and the demand that Muslims participate in both arenas. While the *Qur'an* does not ask believers to forego who they are, it nevertheless says

> We created you from a single (pair) of a male and a female, and made you into Nations and tribes, that you may know each other (not that you may despise each other). Verily the most honored of you in the sight of God is (he who is) the most righteous of you. And God has full knowledge and is well acquainted with all things). (49:13)

In the Qur'anic world view, tribes are created to know one another and to be able to lay their tribal feelings aside at certain times to come together as a large community of believers. In the Qur'anic world view this does not submerge any one community's needs to the needs of another. But even in the days of the Prophet Muhammad, human inclination to put all of its resources into its own kin community predominated.

For Malcolm, knowing that the larger community of Muslims is one of belief and not of nationality does not relieve Muslims of individual accountability and responsibility in their own community. If a Muslim community pursues nation-building (*'asabiya*) and commits all resources (intellectual, spiritual, and physical) it necessarily is marginalized in the larger Muslim world. If a Muslim community sees itself solely as a portion of the world community of belief (*ummah*) and commits its resources there, it forgoes the individual accountability and responsibility to struggle against injustice in its own locale. This is the dilemma Malcolm faced and sought to resolve by incorporating his resources and associates as the Organization of African American Unity, on one hand, and establishing the Muslim Mosque, Inc., on the other.

The contemporary communities (1960–present) further exemplify this tension. Some communities choose *'asabiya* over *ummah*, while other communities struggle with the current realities of participation in *ummah*, which force them to neglect *'asabiya*. In the latter communities, the establishment of Islam as a foundation for nation-building as a priority has given way to the development of Islam in America as a complete worldview. For those communities who choose to have their Islamic expression grounded in *'asabiya*, there is an ongoing tension with those communities who choose a global Islamic perspective.

SUMMARY

At the beginning of the twentieth century, some African Americans unequivocally chose Islam as their worldview in an environment where it was alien to the world view of the majority population. Their embrace of a universal Isalmic worldview was not in immediate conflict with their need to confront America's racism and social injustice. On the contrary, whatever they knew about Islam, all seemed to know that it stood for social justice and personal responsibility.

Leaders were not chosen; rather, leaders formed communities around their conceptualizations of answers to the mental, spiritual, economic, and emotional dilemmas of African Americans. This is important to note, because in the teachings of traditional Sunni Islam, leadership comes from a consensus of the learned regarding who is the most qualified (Sunni) or who in the family of leadership (same blood as Prophet Muhammad) has inherited the internal traits which the upbringing has augmented (Shi'i). But in the specialized case of African American Islam, leadership comes from the faculties of a person who is able to conceptualize possibilities for the life of a people. In African American communities, though solidarity comes to pass as people adhere to the message, the glue is the leader and his gifts.[47]

Historically, Islam comes to already formed cultures, moralizes them, and directs them to the worship of God. For African American leaders, however, nationhood was not pregiven, and their primary concern was building a nation for their oppressed people. This emphasis on nation-building over the universalizing process of Islam risked alienation from the broader family of Islam, but was rationalized by prevailing conditions in America. In subsequent chapters we will return to this fundamental tension between *'asabiya*, African American group solidarity, and *ummah*, solidarity with the broader community of believers. In this context, I would only remark that although an emphasis on nation-building is indeed required in African American Islam, it must not become a never-ending priority which eclipses the fundamental Islamic notion of the community of believers.

Differences between African American Muslim communities hinged on differences between the abilities and orientations of their leaders. Noble Drew Ali was able to see an ostracized African American community that needed to make ties with a heritage. He provided that heritage. After giving some initial guidelines for eating, dress, and moral development, and establishing temples in several cities, he was murdered, leaving the community with two main alternatives. They could either move toward inclusion into the larger Muslim community, or they could retain the guidelines given by Ali and continue emphasizing nation-building. What they actually do we will see in the next chapter.

The Ahmadi movement was guided by systematic Islamic teachings couched in an Indian interpretation on the subcontinent formed in reaction to British colonialism and Hindu elitism and dominance. While this movement gave African American Muslims a level of competency in Islamic and Arabic studies, it lacked a format for dealing with social injustice and racism. Indeed, the missionaries of the movement failed to confront their own racism, and refused to acknowledge internal cultural problems which lead to disillusionment on the part of many African Americans. We will later see what happens as a result of this tension within the movement.

The Nation of Islam, one of the most popular and successful communities, had the potential to become the norm for African American Islamic practice, but this did not happen for at least two decades. What in the environment prevented this from happening for so long? I will attempt to provide some answers to this question in subsequent chapters.

For African American Muslims at the turn of the century, there was a need to focus on the plight of black people in the United States and the daily injustices heaped on them. The tactics and beliefs used to break ties with the larger society were seen as necessary to begin the process of culture formation, as was the designation of a contemporary messenger of God. How these African Americans appropriated Islam to fit their immediate condition and how they perceived what was necessary to change that condition is a story barely unearthed here. That they were able to carve out an Islamic presence in the United States is a testimony to their intellect, courage, and perseverance.

Contemporary Communities 1960 to Present

كِتَٰبٌ أَنزَلْنَٰهُ إِلَيْكَ مُبَٰرَكٌ لِّيَدَّبَّرُوٓا۟ ءَايَٰتِهِۦ وَلِيَتَذَكَّرَ
أُو۟لُوا۟ ٱلْأَلْبَٰبِ ﴿٢٩﴾

(It is) a Book We have revealed to you abounding in good, that they may ponder over its verses, and that those endowed with understanding may be mindful.

—Sura Suad 38:29.

AFRICAN AMERICAN ISLAM in the second half of the twentieth century must be understood within the context of social and political developments both in the United States and in the broader Islamic world. Before examining some contemporary African American Islamic communities, we must therefore discuss some of the events and viewpoints that have helped shape the thought and practice of African American Muslims. Please refer to the Appendix for some of the documents discussed throughout.

Contemporary Communities: 1960 to Present

Moorish Science Temple	R. Love El C. Kirkman Bey
Ahmadiyya Movement	First Pittsburgh Mosque First Cleveland Mosque

Nation of Islam	Nation of Gods and Earths Silis Muhammad John Muhammad Warithudeen Muhammad Louis Farrakhan
Darul Islam	Jamil al-Amin Fuqra
Islamic Party	Muzaffarideen Hamid
Islamic Brotherhood	
United Submitters International	Rashad Khalifa
Shiite Communities	
Ansarullah Nubian Islamic Hebrews	
'Isa al Haadi al Mahdi	
Naqshabandi Community	Sheik Nasim an-Naqshabandi
Tijaniyyah Community	Sheik Hassan Cisse
Addeyuallahe Universal Arabic Association	
Fahamme Temple of Islam and Culture	

REVOLUTIONARY EVENTS AND THE CRISIS IN THE MUSLIM WORLD

During the nineteenth century the Islamic world succumbed to Western Christendom—militarily, economically, and finally, politically. As a result, the very meaning of Muslim history was challenged. What had gone wrong in Islam?[1]

The domination of Islamic lands by the states of western Europe posed a terrible dilemma for Muslims. Why did the divinely ordained Islamic community suffer such defeats at the hands of the infidels? The general

> Muslim consensus was that the divine message revealed to the Prophet remained valid. It was not Islam that was flawed; rather, the flaw lay with Muslims themselves and their failure to follow the commands of God.[2]

In recent decades the world witnessed an explosion of insurgent Muslim activity against Western domination and impingement upon Islamic life. Israeli Olympians were the target of a Palestinian terrorist attack in Munich; there were calls for governments based solely on Islamic law, as Iran moved toward and successfully completed an "Islamic Revolution"; Afghani Muslims waged a successful war against the Soviet Union; the Grand Mosque in Mecca, Saudi Arabia was seized in protest of the Saudi government; and a British author of Indian Muslim descent was sentenced to death by Iran's Ayatollah Khomeni after he scandalized the Prophet of Islam in a novel. These are not the only uprisings or events which took place in the Muslim world during this time, but they are among the most significant in terms of their effect on African American Muslims.

Very little was known about the Shi'i Islam of the Muslims in Iran prior to the Iranian revolution and the hostage crisis. U.S. media representations of Islam were full of pictures vilifying Muslims as "bloodthirsty" savages, wantonly torturing and killing the innocent Americans who worked in the American embassy in Tehran.[3] Veiled Muslim women, always the more visible segment of Muslim communities, were verbally and/or physically assaulted on the streets of urban America. In late 1979 and early 1980 Muslims were viewed as the representatives of Islamic hatred for the "Great Satan" West. According to interviews, however, very few African American Muslims knew anything about issues involved in the Iranian situation. Nor were they particularly knowledgeable about the specifics concerning the Israeli occupation of Palestine. But as a result of the immigration of Muslim Palestinians to the United States, African American Muslims soon had the opportunity to hear the other side of the story in Friday *Jumah* services and social gatherings. Nevertheless, African American Muslims felt the pain that comes with being citizens in a country that supports injustices toward Muslims.

The seizure of the Grand Mosque in Mecca, Saudi Arabia in 1979 was portrayed in the United States media as the ultimate in chaos of "Islamic fundamentalism." Although the event was not widely covered in the press or on the evening news, it nevertheless caused concern in African American Muslim communities. Conversations with Muslims who knew of the seizure revealed confusion and shock that other Muslims would seize the most holy mosque in the Muslim world. Those who were aware of this event were even more surprised that there was at least one African American among the rebels, and they were further amazed at the alleged corruption of the Saudi Arabian government covered in the reports about the attacks on the Grand Mosque.

One other event created a similarly emotional reaction among African Americans. Publication of Salman Rusdie's novel *The Satanic Verses* caused a major uproar in the Muslim world and in the West. Rushdie's novel included an account of the Prophet of Islam's marital life, and cast aspersions on the moral character of his wives (considered by Muslims the "Mothers of Islam"). The author's suggestion that the Prophet was influenced by satanic verses rather than revelation was viewed by the majority of Muslims as blasphemous. In response, the Ayatollah Khomeni offered the formal legal opinion (*fatwa*) that this blasphemy should be punished by death. Writers for the West seized upon the Ayatollah's statement, highlighting the punitive aspect of the *fatwa* as further confirmation of the barbarous nature of Islam, and condemning its willingness to murder rather than permit free speech. In many universities, workplaces, as well as in the press and on national television, American Muslims were put on the spot to declare that they did not share the sentiments of the Muslim world against Rushdie and his text.

Increasingly, throughout the 1970s, 1980s, and 1990s, American Muslims were repeatedly called upon to explain and then denounce "the terrorist activities" of their fellow Muslims in the world.

Global economies, international computer networks, international travels and news have shrunk the world and its events, and the vocabulary propagated by Western media to describe Islam in the second half of the twentieth century—terrorists, fundamentalists, militants, and so on—has been firmly concretized in the minds of many Westerners. These events could not help but have serious effects on African American Islamic communities. African American Muslims had been visible for sixty or more years before the Iranian Revolution, but never before had Muslim women been attacked in the streets of the United States because they looked like the women on the television news who were shouting death to the United States—the "Great Satan." Muslim communities were forced to quickly familiarize themselves with events in the Middle East and North Africa. And as African American Muslims traveled and studied, they have been able in many cases to make more informed decisions about the *ummah* and its agenda. Some communities fully support the Islamic movement over and against the American agenda, while others have moved to more clearly demonstrate their American allegiance.

LITERARY RESPONSES TO THE CRISIS

Scores of Muslim intellectuals emerged to articulate responses to the question of what had "gone wrong" in Islam. In the 1970s and 1980s some of the most influential works in the area were translated into English. Among them were the works of two thinkers who are especially prominent for our discussion—Sayyid Qutb, an Egyptian and Abdul Ala Maududi, an Indian. Both men eschewed wholesale secularism and advocated a committed return to Qur'anic and Islamic studies for guidance and action in the face of European dominance. They also argued that religion must leave the private domain to which colonialism had relegated it and move to the public space, that governments should espouse Islamic ideals, and that Islam as a social force for change must challenge the reigning ideologies of capitalism and communism.

Sayyid Qutb's articulation of "what had gone wrong in Islam" was conveyed to American Muslims primarily in translations of two of his many texts—*Milestones* and *In the Shade of the Qur'an.* Yvonne Haddad, who has written several articles on Qutb, asserts:

> To struggle in the path of God, for Qutb, demands the willingness of the believers to renounce egotistical achievements and individual goals. The primary goal should be the corporate benefit, the *ummah* living in righteousness under the law of God.[4]

As Haddad's remark indicates, Qutb calls upon Muslims to reaffirm their commitment to Islam as a priority. Moreover, he expressly addresses issues regarding nationality, race, and family, which are of particular importance to African American Muslims.

> The distinctive feature of a Muslim Community is this: that in all its affairs it is based upon worship of God alone.[5]

> There is only one place on earth that can be called the home of Islam (Darul-Islam) and it is that place where the Islamic state is established. . . . The rest of the world is the home of hostility (Darul-Harb).[6]

> Divine relationship does not prohibit a Muslim from treating his parents with kindness and consideration, in spite of differences of belief, as long as they do not join the front lines of the enemies of Islam.[7]

> Islam cannot accept any mixing with *jahiliyyah* (doctrine that runs contrary to revelation), either in its concept or modes of living which are derived from this concept.[8]

Abdul Ala Maududi's thought elaborates a similar conceptualization. As the founder of Jam'at-i-Islami, the most influential Muslim organization in South Asia, Maududi

> explained his purpose as twofold: 1) to expose the nature of *jahiliyyah* and all the evil that it contains especially in its modern Western form; and 2) to present the Islamic way of life in a reasoned, argued, demonstrated, and systematic fashion.[9]

> These people should pause for a while and consider as best they can the following question: Are they prepared to face the natural and logical consequences of the Western way of life which have already appeared in Europe and America? Do they really want: that their social environment also should be charged with sexual and emotional excitements? that their nation also should abound in immodesty, corruption and sexual promiscuity?[10]

Jahiliyyah refers to the recurring state of ignorance in which humankind is self-indulgent, prideful, and blasphemous. For both Qutb and Maududi, this was the West. Westernization spreads, along with technology, and corruption of the moral fabric of society. For Qutb, the process was the antithesis of Islam. In his society (Egyptian), the post-colonial state's push toward secularism was suicide. For many African American Muslims, sitting in the middle of what was identified as *jahiliyyah*, the necessary response was the need to separate. If separation was not immediately possible, then the believer should attempt to reconstruct where he/she lived to the model of the earliest community, in both appearance and in discipline.

> There would be a break between the Muslim's present Islam and his past *Jahiliyyah*, and this after a well thought out decision, as a result of which all his relationships with *Jahiliyyah* would be cut off and he would be joined completely to Islam, although there would be some give-and-take with the polytheists in commercial activity and daily business; yet relationships of understanding are one thing and daily business is something else.
>
> We must also free ourselves from the clutches of *jahili* society, *jahili* concepts, *jahili* traditions and *jahili* leadership. Our mission is not to compromise with the practices of *jahili* society, nor can we be loyal to it . . . . Our aim is first to change ourselves so that we may later change society.[11]

The powerful messages and straightforward styles, along with earnest appeals and simplification of the goals of Islam, made the translated works of these two leaders very attractive to readers in the United States. As a result these texts were heavily relied upon for interpretation of both the *Qur'an* and the proper Islamic life. Supporters of Qutb and Maududi have written scores of texts disseminating their thoughts around the world, and these works have become the mainstay of knowledge for Muslims in the United States. (Prior to the dissemination of these texts, many Muslims in the United States were getting their information orally rather than through reading.)

At present, educational levels of African American Muslims are steadily increasing, leading them to seek out a wider range of Islamic literature and to publish some of it themselves. There is also a greater frequency of travel to the Muslim world for hajj and for study—leading to the beginnings of a community of African American Muslim scholars.

INFLUENCES FROM THE CIVIL RIGHTS AND BLACK POWER MOVEMENTS

In 1955 in Montgomery, Alabama, southern blacks responded to an incident over segregated buses with a boycott. Enlisting the assistance of local ministers, the boycott organized and spread to other southern cities. With this boycott Dr. Martin Luther King, Jr. emerged as the leader of what was shortly to become a massive "application of civil disobedience" that lasted until his death in 1968. On 1 February 1960, four black college students in Greensboro, North Carolina, added another aspect to a growing refusal to accommodate segregation by sitting down at a segregated lunch counter and waiting to be served.

Freedom rides and protest marches throughout the South pricked the consciousness of the nation as all of these events and the violence of the local law enforcement agencies was witnessed on national television. For almost a decade, northern white social activists and mostly southern blacks risked (and sometimes lost) their lives to protest the nation's refusal to guarantee the rights of its black citizens. For at least eight years, the television news was an endless picture of dogs and baton-wielding police attacking unarmed black and white protesters. The "March on Washington" in 1963 and the subsequent Voting Rights Act of 1965 were the most visible results of this effort. The 1968 assassination of Martin

Luther King, Jr. confirmed in the minds of many the intrinsic racism in the United States. Violence erupted in 110 cities across the nation.[12]

Frustrated and disillusioned with nonviolent protest, some members of the civil rights movement—central leaders of the Student Nonviolent Coordinating Committee (SNCC)—agitated for a different kind of struggle. As Clayborne Carson writes, this

> began a new stage in the transformation of Afro-American political consciousness. Shattering the fragile alliance of civil-rights forces, the black power upsurge challenged the assumptions underlying previous interracial efforts to achieve national civil rights reforms.[13]

During this time Stokely Carmichael and Hubert "Rap" Brown emerged as leaders who "argued for the cultural and political autonomy of black communities."[14] Raising political consciousness another step became a full-time job under a different title—black power. Advocating political activism and independence rather than integration, the black power movement forced violent confrontations with white groups across the nation in the late 1960s and 1970s. Carmichael and Charles V. Hamilton articulated some of the central ideology of the movement as follows:

> The values of this society support a racist system; we find it incongruous to ask black people to adopt and support most of those values. We also reject the assumption that the basic institutions of this society must be preserved. The goal of black people is not to be assimilated into middle-class America, for that class—as a whole—is without a viable conscience as regards humanity.[15]

Malcolm X, Stokely Carmichael, H. Rap Brown, Huey Newton, Maulana Karenga and a host of others spoke to the needs of African Americans to become actors, to provide for themselves, and to become citizens with power.

This text will not elaborate on all of various political and cultural positions taken by African Americans during these decades. Some of these positions, however, are especially important in the political and cultural stances of African American Muslims, who span the range from accomodationist/integrationist to cultural-nationalist.

It is difficult to assess the specific influence of the civil rights movement on African American Islam. Some African American Muslims speak of having been activists prior to becoming Muslim, but not after. The influences of the black power movement, however, are most readily seen in the ideologies of various communities. Many communities place an emphasis, though not a priority, on their heritage, on the need to express that heritage in dress and social etiquette, and express a disdain for the West and Christianity. For some communities, the influence of the black power movement is seen in refusals to join the armed forces, salute the flag, sing the national anthem, and other public displays of patriotism. These acts however, also are strongly influenced by Islamic understandings. Perhaps the lack of influence of the civil rights movement was largely due to its Christian base.

Nevertheless, in noting this broad influence of the black power movement in comparison to the civil rights movement, we must be careful to avoid the fallacious conclusion that African American Islam is only or "at bottom" a nationalistic movement. C. Eric Lincoln has cautioned against this fallacy, while citing some of the causes that perpetuate such a conclusion:

> Because black ethnicity and black identity are often expressed through black religion, black religion is often mistaken for black nationalism. Black nationalism is a political philosophy.

> Its goals, which are amorphous by design, do not give primary consideration to man's spiritual quest, even though religion may appear as the focus of its activities.[16]

As Lincoln's remark clearly suggests, to interpret African American Islam primarily in terms of its nationalist elements would, at best, amount to a distorting oversimplification.

CONTEMPORARY AFRICAN AMERICAN MUSLIM COMMUNITIES

The second half of this century has witnessed an explosion of Muslim communities in the United States. As of this writing, there are at least seventeen distinct communities of Islamic expression. These communities can be differentiated in terms of (1) Islamic understanding—how they adhere to what has come to be known in the Sunni Muslim world as the five pillars: *shahada* (affirmation of belief) *salat* (five-times-daily prayers), *zakat* (obligatory sharing of excess wealth), *sawm* (fasting), and *hajj* (pilgrimage to Mecca); (2) whether the group has nation-building as its focus rather than the wider Muslim community (here and abroad); and (3) how they acknowledge the leader of the community—as divinely inspired (i.e., as *mahdi* or messiah), as the most learned, or as some combination of the two.

Members of the nascent groups engaged in the process of propagating and spreading their influence without fanfare. One source of Islamic propagation among African Americans was in the world of music.[17] African American musicians frequently had to emigrate to Europe to realize their successes, and a surprisingly significant number were Muslims. Their European experiences with Muslims from all over the world clarified and augmented their Islamic knowledge and their choices of Islamic practices.

Muhammad Speaks, the newspaper of the Nation of Islam, was also instrumental in the growth of African American Islam, as it served to bridge the gap in knowledge about Africans, African Americans and the rest of the world. One example of the kind of information it provided is recorded by Karl Evanzz:

> On November 22, 1963, *Muhammad Speaks* became the only publication in America to reprint China's Chairman Mao Zedong's letter of encouragement to CORE director James Farmer, who was in a Louisiana jail on charges stemming from his efforts to end segregation there. "I ask the workers, peasants, revolutionary intellectuals, sensitive bourgeoisie elements and other sensitive persons of all colors of the world—black, white, yellow, brown—to unite against the racial discrimination of U.S. imperialism and to support the Negro Americans in their fight against racial discrimination," Mao wrote.[18]

It was through the African American print media that the general African American community was made aware of some of the atrocities committed by the United States. In Africa, as nations struggled for independence from colonial rule and its hegemony, *Muhammad Speaks*, *Sepia* and, on rare occasions, *Jet* magazine kept black people informed and angry. *Muhammad Speaks* almost single-handedly took on the charge of investigating activities against African leaders who did not wish to continue to permit the United States to continue its exploitation of their resources.

During the early 1960s the Oriental Exclusion Act was repealed and large numbers of foreign Muslims began to immigrate to the United States. In 1963 the Muslim Students Association was organized by students at the University of Illinois and quickly spread to campuses all over the United States. This organization, which publishes several magazines and disseminates Islamic literature, was also a major influence on African American Muslim communities. Foreign Muslim students were frequent visitors in these communities, sometimes providing classes in various Islamic disciplines. Islamic centers began to spring up in all the major cities. Both Sunni and Shiite Muslims used the same *masaajid* (mosques), so few persons in the African American communities, until very recently, would have noticed any differences between these two groups. The 1960s also witnessed a surge in the actual building of *masaajid* in the United States.

During this time, the embassies of several Muslim countries such as Saudi Arabia, Pakistan, Egypt, Libya, and the Sudan made available free copies of Yusef Ali's translation of the *Holy Qur'an* and vast amounts of Islamic literature and pamphlets to the American public. A large number of African American communities also had English-speaking Egyptian or Pakistani Imams (leaders of prayer and in general the community) in residence, and had frequent visits from traveling *jama'ats* (groups or communities of educators) more popularly known as *tablighi jama'ats.*[19] The volume of Islamic literature, albeit only of a certain kind, increased a hundredfold. It is significant for subsequent discussion to recognize that the literature that made its way to the African American communities was primarily from Pakistan and Egypt.

The Moorish Science Temple of America

> We are friends and servants of humanity. We are dedicated to the purpose of elevating the moral, social and economic status of our people. We have set about to do this through a wide and comprehensive program embodying the principles of love, truth, peace, freedom and justice.[20]

It is estimated that today there are approximately ten thousand members of the Moorish Science Temple in fifteen cities across the United States. Since the initial leadership of Noble Drew Ali there have arisen several strands of power within the Moorish-American community. The primary power-bases center on the leadership of C. Kirkmon Bey and John Givens-El. C. Kirkmon Bey was Ali's secretary and an elected leader, while John Givens-El is asserted to be a reincarnation of Ali. Offices continue to be masonic in titles and job descriptions. The Moorish-American community is one of only two communities that have women in positions of leadership. The Young People's Moorish National League and the Moorish National Sisters Auxiliary, both established in 1928, continue. There are several Moors still living from the days of the first community, including Sister Pearl Ali, wife of Noble Drew Ali.

Interviews with members of this community in Chicago, Pittsburgh, Philadelphia, and St. Louis were very informative. Both men and women were hospitable and engaging. They were very supportive of any telling of the story of their community and wanted to clear up misconceptions—such as the one which asserts that they were not "really Muslim." Although they are still using masonic titles for offices, they have incorporated a substantial amount of Islamic vocabulary into their everyday conversations. When asked about whether or not the community members observed the core obligations of Islamic worship, the Grand Sheik in St. Louis responded that "the way the community was set up made these observances an individual responsibility."

Moorish-American Muslims clearly consider themselves members of the large family of Muslims, although Noble Drew Ali left them few guidelines with regard to the practice of the faith, and there is no evidence in their literature that anyone has focused attention on these matters. The Moors celebrate the Prophet's (Noble Drew Ali's) Birthday, January 8; New Year, January 15; and Flag Day in August. Ramadan is not celebrated by the entire community, but it is celebrated by individuals—sometimes even with other Muslim communities. Drinking in public and smoking are forbidden, and Moors are strongly encouraged not to eat pork.

Some members pray three times daily (others do not pray formally), but this prayer is performed while standing, and does not conform in content to the *salat.* Charity is given primarily within the community, but *zakat* is not an established practice.

The collective community of Moors publishes several papers—the *Moorish Guide National Edition* (established in 1928); *Moorish Science Monitor* (probably first published in the 1960s, stopped in 1966, and resumed in 1986); *Moorish Scribe* (1970s); *Moorish Review* (1950–1960s); *Moorish Voice* (1970s–1980s); and *Moorish-American Voice* (1990s). Recently, Moors can be seen on cable television networks and have produced one-half to one-hour segments propagating their philosophy. At the time of this writing, a renewed campaign to attract new members to the community is underway.

Although Moorish-American Muslims vigorously assert the need to uphold the United States Constitution and the laws of the land, they strongly adhere to the Holy Prophet Noble Drew Ali's "Divine Mission" to "uplift fallen humanity," and are still actively proclaiming that the issue of nationality is critical to any self-understanding among ex-slaves in the United States. Such nationalism is evident in a petition signed and submitted by one Moorish community to the United States Congress in 1985, which calls for the restoration of a Moorish Nation with congressional recognition of the Moorish-American national name. As security for their community, the Moors are struggling to achieve economic security. Toward this end, the Moorish Uplifting Fund, the new form of the Great Moorish Treasury, continues to grow. The original Moorish products such as tonic, mineral salts, and so on, continue to be manufactured and sold from their temples.

Moorish-American Muslims have always claimed to be neither integrationists nor separatists, but demand that Moors maintain their own nationality and act as a nation. Steadfast in their belief that Noble Drew Ali is a Prophet, teacher, reformer and redeemer of American ex-slaves who have been deceived of their true nationality, Moors persist in the latter half of the twentieth century in positioning themselves for growth.

The Ahmadiyya Muslim Community

Building on the mission Dr. Hazrat Mufti Muhammad Sadiq began in 1920, the Ahmadiyya Muslim community continued to be a very influential community among African Americans until the early part of the 1980s. The movement has been especially noted for its increase in social-service programs across the country. In recent years, however, the movement has lost some of its prominence, due to the growth of Sunni Islam in America, and the concomitant legal opinion by Islamic officials on the Indian subcontinent that the Ahmadi were a heretical group. In 1974, the government of Pakistan declared the movement heretical, and the Sunni Muslim majority began to persecute the community, causing an increase in Pakistani Ahmadi immigration to the United States. This influx shifted the ethnic balance of the Ahmadiyya community in the United States from predominantly African American to predominantly Pakistani.

The Ahmadiyya *jama'ats* have spent a great deal of energy clarifying their position in Islam for the benefit of both interested non-Muslims and other American Muslims who are unclear about the controversy. Toward this end, there are numerous pamphlets and texts which address the Ahmadiyya understanding on various Muslim issues.[21] This community has become very explicit in elaborating its fundamental beliefs in the *Qur'an*, the *Sunnah* (Way) of the Prophet Muhammad, and the five pillars.

By 1991 the Ahmadiyya Muslim community could claim ten million adherents in more than 120 countries. In the United States, the Ahmadiyya Muslim community branches are established in thirty-eight cities, with eight *masajid* and thirty-eight mission houses, and the numbers are growing. Organization is a typical emphasis in this community, and it revolves around the system of Khalafat.[22] An electoral college from members of the community elects a Khalifah by majority vote. As the religious leader of the community, the Khalifah directs all of the affairs of the community in accordance with Islamic principles. The Khalifah requires a *bai'at* (pledge of allegiance) from the community members to reaffirm their allegiance to him and the cause of Islam.[23] There is an appointed national leader (*amir*), and elected presidents at the local level.

Each local community is organized around age and gender groups: Nasirats (girls ages 7–16), Young Lajna (young women ages 16–21), Khuddam ul-Ahmadiyya (men ages 15–40), Lajna (women over 21), and Ansar (men over 40). These associations each function according to a constitution and a yearly, nationally-standardized, program that is given to each community around the world by the Khalifah. Each community's program is focused around worship, education, and service to humanity. Ahmadi service programs include food and clothing programs and programs for Muslims in dire circumstances in the United States and abroad. Non-Ahmadi Muslims can call upon the Ahmadi community for assistance and, at present, the Ahmadi have a very extensive aid program for Bosnian refugees. One sister who is a national office holder in the community asserted: "These service programs are not bound to the Ahmadi propagation effort but rather are seen as part of their pledge to serve humanity."

The local president, referred to as a missionary, receives training abroad, where study focuses on Arabic, *tafsir* (commentary), *Shari'ah* (Islamic law), and *Kalam* (conversation about God). The position/status of missionary gives a person the required knowledge to convey the message and confers eligibility to lead a community. Several African Americans have attempted to pursue this course of study, but at this time only one has been successful—Dr. Hanif, who is a missionary in California. (At this writing Dr. Hanif has just been appointed a missionary in Chicago, Illinois. He will assume his duties in Chicago in the fall of 1994.) Members of this community expressed concern over finding ways to make the training more accessible or at least more feasible. Although African Americans in this group are probably the most widely traveled, as they have fellow communities around the world, this once influential community has not been successful in attracting African Americans in recent decades.

The Five Percenters: The Nation of Gods and Earths

> Our Father Allah taught the pimps, pushers, hookers to become the wisest people in the universe. He always taught the young.

In New York in 1964, Clarence 13X founded the Five Percenters after leaving the Nation of Islam and distributing the Nation of Islam's "Lost-Found Muslim Lessons." These lessons, it has been reported, contain

> the basic elements of an ancient mystery school. It involved secrecy from outsiders; an esoteric ritual containing keys for recognition between fellow members; a cohesive worldview; and a tradition that could be explained only to initiates. Central to these teachings were the knowledge of self and the black man's god head.[24]

The Five Pecenters derived their name from the following conception of the populace: The Five Percent were those who taught righteousness, freedom, justice, and equality to all the human family. The Eighty-Five Percent, the masses, believed in a "mystery God" and worshipped "that which did not exist." The Ten Percent were the "bloodsuckers" of the poor who taught the Eighty-Five Percent that a mystery God existed. The Five Percent were destined to be poor, righteous teachers and to struggle successfully against the Ten Percent . . . to lead the Eighty-Five Percent to freedom, justice, and equality.

Originally called the Five Percent Nation of Islam, this group emphasized the 120 lessons that W. D. Fard Muhammad taught and the 150 questions that he asked and Elijah Muhammad answered. By the time Clarence 13X was murdered on 13 June 1969, he had established a group of the "First Born" to carry on the teachings of the group. The youth he taught gave him the name "Father Allah." Since he had taught against centralized leadership, believing it made a community vulnerable—if the leader dies the message dies—there is no definitive leadership after his death, nor is there any organizational structure to point out.

Five Percenters adhere to the concept of the diversity of man, which states that each man has a certain rate at which he learns. They also believe that when a man has learned his lessons he achieves the status of a god and is given a divine name. The Five Percenters are now known as the Nation of Gods and Earths—Earths are the female members. The teachings of the Nation of Gods and Earths revolve around nine principles. According to Father Lord Lael Great Mind Allah, these principles are:

1. Black people are the original people of the planet Earth.
2. Black people are our fathers and mothers of civilization.
3. The Science of divine math is the key to understanding man's relationship to the universe.
4. Islam is a natural way of life, not a religion.
5. Education should be fashioned to make us self-sufficient as a people.
6. Each one should teach one according to their knowledge.
7. Blackman is God and his proper name is Allah (Arm, Leg, Leg, Arm, Head).
8. Our children are our link to the future and they must be nurtured, respected, loved, protected and educated.
9. The unified Black family is the vital building block of the Nation.[25]

The nation has parliament rallies on the last Sunday of each month, where the community comes together to learn of new knowledge and books.

> We meet for the congregation to come together to deal with perfect equality, speak a universal language that is mathematics, and share our knowledge, wisdom and understanding amongst one another so that we can grow as a Nation.[26]

The Show and Prove is held each year on the second Sunday in June to commemorate the birth of their leader.

Women, referred to as Earths, learn who they are and their proper place from the men. In general, the woman's role is "to learn to keep children, home and be there for her man."[27] She is also taught proper behavior for home and abroad. Women can have a profession and a career; this is an avenue for spreading understanding. Women are to be fully covered, wearing face veils with unadorned skin (no cosmetics are used). There are no dowries or church weddings, but most members have civil ceremonies.

The community publishes five monthly newsletters: *Builders Always Build, The Word, The Son of Man, The Foundation,* and *God on Point,* which are available at the monthly parliament meeting. The group is spread around the United States, with the largest base in New York, where Manhattan is known as Mecca, Brooklyn as Medina, Queens as the Desert, Bronx as Pelan, and Nassau County as Lord's Islands. Several well-known rap artists, including Lakim Shabazz, are members of the Nation of Gods and Earths.

Ansarullah Nubian Islamic Hebrews

> The Ansaru Allah Community are propagators of true Islaam in the West. We are not nationalists, imperialists, nor pseudo–Islamic. We are

> "Ansarullah" (Aiders of Allah–Al-Qur'aan 3:152), or "peacemakers" (Matthew 5:9, Al-Qur'aan 22:78) who dress in the garb of the righteous (Revelations 3:5, Al-Qur'aan 61:14) and have taken the duty to spread true Islam.[28]

The Ansarullah community, led by As-Sayyid Isa Al Haadi and based in New York until very recently, has branch communities across the United States and throughout the world.[29] Continually publishing since 1971, this community has disseminated well over two hundred books, almost three hundred cassette tapes and dozens of video tapes, along with a newspaper and hundreds of information flyers.[30] In its research department, this community archives articles and texts on numerous African American organizations and communities. Many rhythm-and-blues, rap, and pop musicians have had their start on labels owned and recorded in this community's studio. The community also has its own singing groups. From its publications, distinctive dress, and nationwide network of vendors, members of communities that follow Imam Isa's leadership have become well known.

Pooling their resources, efforts, and experiences, the Ansaar live communally, with collective ownership and control of property and goods. This is seen as mandatory in order to live the prescribed way of life, and in order to remain separate from disbelievers. In this community, members worship together under the guidance of a kind of house mother, and generally speak only Arabic. Teachers are employed from Morocco, Egypt, Sudan, and Mali. Regarding the education of children, Imam Isa writes:

> In their early years of learning, we concentrate on teaching them the language of Qur'aan (Arabic *Fusha*). When they reach the age of understanding they are introduced to the Ansaru Allah doctrine.[31]

Female children are taught "cooking, sewing, weaving, housekeeping, dance, music, accounting, Islamic culture and customs. Children begin to learn to make formal prayers at the age of four years, four months and four days.[32]

Among the many distinguishing and unique assertions of this community is Imam Isa's proclaimed Sudanese ancestry and teachings concerning the place of Nubians in world history. He says that he is a member of the Mahdi family,[33] and he has insisted on traditional Sudanese dress for members of the community. Women in this community wear a full bodice covering and also cover their faces, exposing only their eyes. The men wear Sudanese style *jalabiya* and head coverings. The community is called Nubian because:

> we descended from the Prophet Noah through Cush (Genesis 10:6), who was the father of Nuba, called Nubia. Nubia covered part of what is now Sudan, and extended along the Nile River from the Southern boundary of Ancient Egypt almost to present day Khartoum, Sudan.[34]

The reference to Hebrews in the community's name derives from an association with Abraham:

> Al Islaam is our way of life. It is not a new way of life; on the contrary, it is a continuation of the religion of the Prophet Abraham and the complete overall laws for the universal government and the guidance of Prophet Abraham's seed.[35]

From the beginning of his community, Imam Isa has been anti–Saudi Arabian. He has leveled charges of racism and "sectism" against Arabs in each and every text and newspaper of the community. Jews and Europeans also receive a great deal of Imam Isa's hostility, as do African–American Muslims who work with them or Arabs in any position. Claiming to "question everything" Imam Isa has produced a veritable library of information on just about every issue ever raised in discussion among African American Muslims.

Imam Isa is an ardent supporter of the teachings of Elijah Muhammad, though he makes no claims of kinship. He also claims that "Shaikh Dauod Ahmed Faisal passed on the Islamic Mission in America's Charter to him and that he carries on that work." Some time after 1990, Imam Isa changed his name and that of his community. He is now known as the Rabbani Y'shua Bar El Haady and calls his group "The Saviors" with headquarters in Atlanta, Georgia. There are now no references to Allah but to Yahuwa Eloh. His latest works serve to give foundation to the new community and to question what he calls the orthodoxy of Sunni Muslims.

The Islamic Party of North America: The Community Mosque

Motto of the The Islamic Party of North America:

> Allah is our Lord
> Muhammad is our Leader
> Qur'an is Our Guide
> Sunnah is Our Ideal
> Jehad is Our Means
> Salvation is Our End.
>
> The real objective of Islam is emancipation of man from the slavery of man, of nation from the bondage of nation and of humanity from the yoke of humanity, and to turn the whole of mankind into one free brotherhood consisting of the servants of one God who created them.[36]

During the 1960s Yusuf Muzaffaruddin Hamid journeyed to the Muslim world to study with Hizabutkria, Maadsumi, Ihkwan

Muslimoon, the Jamaati Islami, and the Said Nursi Movement. He finished his studies as a house guest of Abul A'la Maududi in Pakistan. Returning to Washington, D.C. in 1969, Imam Yusuf found no masjid for the people in the city except the Islamic Center (formerly the Islamic Culture Center Museum) on Embassy Row. Along with a small group of committed Muslim men and women, Imam Yusuf "saw the need for an independent mosque in the D.C. ghetto because it was directly affected by the basic problems of human rights, social justice, economic degradation and racism."[37] He thus founded the Islamic Party of North America in 1971 in order "to facilitate the sharing and understanding of the Islamic way of life, and teaching Muslims their prayers while sharing with them programs which Islamized their lifestyles."[38]

These statements formed the core of understanding for community activity. Using *sirah* literature (literature that focuses on the early Muslim community and the person of the Prophet Muhammad), they ascertained the basic steps for beginning a community: rally the people around the concept of *tauheed* (the unity of God); do not initially attack prevalent social evils; and give attention first to establishing the proper basis of life. The prevailing notion was that people will always consider a message on the strength and example of its adherents. Personal examples are seen as the actual embodiment of a message.

The Islamic Party moved to concretize its community by quickly publishing a newspaper, *Al-Islam*, a newsletter *The Islamic Party in North America News*, and two books: *Organization in Islam* and *Ad-Da'wah: The Islamic Call*. Among the priorities on the agenda was a constitution. *Organization in Islam* focused on Islam's organized worship as the paradigm to follow.

> O you who believe . . . hold tight to the rope of Allah in an organized way, and do not cause one another to be separated.[39]

Organization and slow, gradual internalization of the message was the way. The Party established the Community Mosque as an incorporated entity with an amirate, Imams, and a *Majlis Shura* (advisory council) on a national level, with primary branch communities in Pittsburgh, Chicago, Virginia, New Jersey, Maryland, and Georgia forming a federation. Initially, the primary focus was on the morality of the community.

> It is essential that these people develop and sustain a dynamic moral strength in their liberation struggle. Moral strength itself has the inherent ability, when applied, of actually changing mental conditions.[40]

Although the Party initially concentrated on the "moral reformation" of its members, it provided ideological stances for the community with regard to the reigning political ideologies of the African American community, other African American Muslims, and the black power movement.

> The party is based on the firm conviction that Islam is an all-pervading and comprehensive "Order of Life" which it intends to promulgate and translate into action in all spheres of human life. The party believes that the root cause of all troubles in man's life is forgetfulness of Allah (God) Almighty, his disregard of Divine Guidance as revealed through the Prophets and his lack of concern for being accountable for his deeds in the Hereafter. . . . Without bringing about this fundamental change, every attempt to reform society on the basis of any of the materialistic concepts of justice (Racism, Nationalism, Capitalism, Communist-Marxism, etc.), will only result in other forms of injustice.[41]

The party also directed energy to neighborhood cleanup drives, and to neighborhood classes in crafts, sewing, and hygiene. The Party had prison programs, martial art classes, boy scout troops, and large food drives. Coming into being at a time when Americans had successfully demonstrated their anger against American involvement in Vietnam, the Party took a strong position with regard to the military. Their position asserted:

> In tune with this practical guidance we have evolved a policy on Muslim participation in Armed Forces, which is intended to instruct both the Muslim and non-Muslim people in this nation of the positive morality behind Muslims' not participating in unjust wars as it would obstruct the true worship of ALLAH and subsequently make the Muslim part of a thing in which he places no stock.[42]

In an interview concerning the beliefs and achievements of the Islamic Party, Yusuf Muzafaraddin Hamid, a founder and leader of the Party, offered several key observations about the Party:

> 1. I believe that the Islamic Party was the first national *jaamat*, to my recollection, that put forward a clear program in writing. It was a constitutional organization. . . . it took leadership out of the category of personality. . . we made it clear that the leader of the Party was just the leader of the organization.
> 2. I believe that the question of dawah facilitating understanding of Islam would be another area of achievement of the Party. The

> Islamic Party was constitutionally mandated to work for the establishment of the Deen (Islamic way of life), the Deen of ALLAH.
>
> 3. I want to emphasize that while dawah was a very important part of our program, the training, the discipline of the minds, spirits and character of our members was of equal, if not more value.[43]

After the *Qur'an* and *hadith*, Qutb's *Milestones* has been a guiding ideology for the Islamic Party with regard to living in America. The Party understood its task as twofold: to establish Islam in America, and to nurture the level of morality prescribed by the *Qur'an*. *Milestones* had defined *Jahiliyyah* and its evils and affirmed the necessity of living apart from the corruption. Years after the formal organization disbanded and Muzzafarradin had established a small community in northern Georgia, the major assertions of *Milestones* were still its guiding philosophy, but with the understanding of the particularities of living in America. In a dinner conversation two years before his death from leukemia in late 1991 or early 1992, Hamid asserted:

> There is a review needed, since 1972, of the political process. We've got to review *Milestones* in its context. . . . Everything has its context . . . even the *Qur'an*. . . . we all have this burning desire to live under an Islamic authority. The methodologies of the Jamati-Islami and the Ikwan . . . are not working. Peoples' minds are being worked on. . . . I am suggesting that we need a much higher degree of spirituality in our life.[44]

With reference to past programs to establish Islam in the inner city through community work, Hamid remarked,

> Isn't the sum total of our whole argument that we are victims of *jahiliyhah*? . . . We must move to protect and defend Muslims. . . . We need a big piece of land. . . . We can commute for money.[45]

Darul Islam (The Abode of Islam)

> In the name of Allah, the Gracious, the Merciful; Allah is the Greatest; Bearing witness that there is god but Allah and that Muhammad (peace be upon him) is His messenger, and being a follower of the last prophet and Messenger of Allah, I hereby pledge myself to the Shariah and to those who are joined by this pledge, I pledge myself, by pledging my love, energy, wealth, life and life and abilities. I also pledge myself to the *maglis* (Imammate), whose duty is to establish, develop, defend and govern according to the precepts of the Shariah.[46]

Accounts of the beginnings of Darul Islam say it began on Atlantic Avenue in Brooklyn, New York in 1962, as a result of the efforts of Ishaq Abduga Shaheed, Rajab Mahmu, and Yahya Abdul-Kareem. With branch communities in major cities across America, Darul Islam is now considered by many African American Muslims to be the most influential African American Islamic philosophy. It is a philosophy which makes literal use of the *Qur'an* and *hadith*. The influence of this movement can be seen in the number of persons having had intimate and formative contact with the movement over its history. Original charter members and, later, general members tended to be ex–cultural nationalists from the black power movement. Membership is awarded on the basis of demonstrated ability to learn the information contained in the *Fundamentals of Islam*, a study book developed by Shaykh Dauod for the training of new members.

The Dar is a very private group. Its privacy is demonstrated by the fact that new members are required to earn their way into the core of the community over a period of time. In the Dar Central community in Philadelphia, prospective members were first queried in a kind of anteroom to the main masjid facilities. The focus of the questioning was the motivation for the initiate's desire to join the movement. Later, they might be invited to attend Sunday classes talking about Islam. Muslims who were not members could not even gain access to *Jumah salat* without proof of a valid reason for doing so.

As mentioned above, training and community life is based upon a literal use of the *Qur'an* and *hadith*. The Dar have their own book for community members, and each member has to memorize its contents before they can give their *shahadah* (profession of faith). After a test based on a study book, one's *bai'at* (pledge of allegiance to the leader) must be given and accepted. There are classes to assist with memorization of the orientation book, and teachers are appointed for *ta'lim* classes (classes on general Islamic topics).

The Dar movement has a *majlis ash-shurah* or governing body from constituency communities, which makes decisions for the membership. The movement is very hierarchical in structure. The leadership is selected on the traditional criterion of being "most knowledgeable" of the *Qur'an* and the *hadith*. The entire community has drills wherein various skills—recitation of the *Qur'an*, fitness, martial arts, and so on—are competitively tested. Community members, both men and women, participate in challenging survival excursions into uninhabited areas. Every woman learns how to sew, and cook fresh game from scratch. Young males are enlisted in *jawalallah* scout troops, in which non-Muslim youths and youths from other Muslim communities participate. At these retreats, youths learn drills, martial arts, survival skills, horseback riding, and so on. Within the movement, there is a heavy emphasis on learning Arabic, and many members complete as many as ten or fifteen years of Arabic training. Men and women who have studied overseas teach these classes.

The Dar movement has never been very open to immigrant communities. Members of other Sunni communities can become affiliate members, but this class of membership does not afford access to the movement's center. Gender separation is strictly observed in congregational prayers, with women sitting on a separate floor on Fridays. Polygamy is extensively practiced, and most women do not work. Resources for the construction and/or purchase of masajid are therefore provided by the men. No facility that is to be used as a masjid can be prayed in until it is completely paid for. Members are encouraged to live nearby places of worship. Businesses are nominal within the community, though the membership is employed to a significant percentage, and lists skilled union members and licensed professionals in its ranks.

At the central or headquarters community, women usually wear full *hijab* (face coverings). The subject of the *Jumah salat* is generally *Taqwa*—Allah consciousness or variations upon that theme. Imams are the persons who have demonstrated the better grasp of the language and content of the *Qur'an*, *hadith*, and the skills of effective communication. In further efforts to live according to the *sunnah*, families acquire very little in household furnishings (wardrobes are sparse but serviceable), and adhere to the traditions of "moral dress" (men wear long baggy pants and shirts, women wear long, loose clothing with a veil). For Friday's *Jumah salat*, the preferred color of dress, for both men and women is white for purity. Full face veils adorn many of the women at these services. (In recent years, some men have begun to wear African dress while women have stopped wearing *hijab*.)

The *majlis* (governing body) handles all internal matters of the community. There is a private masjid-based school, and the public school system generally is not used. Key relationships such as marriages are recorded under the auspices of *Qur'an*ic injunctions. This is less so the farther the community is from the core center of the movement. Some records are maintained on such crucial areas. Divorces and child support decrees are also recorded.

As a philosophy, the Dar movement, more so than any of the other groups discussed here, may be the most difficult to describe. There is no leader to focus on whose thought forms the movement's glue. The Imams of the movement are those best qualified to lead the *salah.* Dar members populate various masajid throughout the country, but they are generally not distinctly labeled as Dar communities. Like the Ansarullah community, the Dar community is not limited to the American continent.

In the late 1970s, an Indian Muslim by the name of Shaykh Jalani entered the Dar movement and convinced two of its founders and a significant number of members to form a community called the Fuqra. The tenants of the Dar are still viable as a movement within Islam, with increasing numbers of *hufaz* (memorizers) of *Qur'an,* scholars,and other members in recent years.

The Nation of Islam: Wallace D. Muhammad and the World Community of Islam in the West

With the "First Official Interview with the Supreme Minister of the Nation of Islam, The Honorable Wallace D. Muhammad,"[47] a fundamental transition within the world of the Nation of Islam began. With an understanding that his role was that of *mujeddid* (one to watch over the new Islam; reviver), Mr. Muhammad initiated a profound and exceedingly complex process of Islamic growth. Muslims in this community continued to understand themselves as part of the world community of Islam, but they also saw themselves as an independent Muslim community among other independent Muslim communities.[48]

In *Lectures of Emam Muhammad,* published in 1978, a significant elaboration of the epistemological underpinnings of the Nation of Islam appeared. In this text, Imam Muhammad deemphasizes the "actual facts" that had been the mainstay of knowledge in the Nation of Islam,[49] displacing some of the central foundational "truths" of the Nation. Imam Muhammad begins by focusing on the notion that Fard Muhammad (the founder of the movement) was God in person. First, he states all the names that have been given to the Honorable Master Fard Muhammad—such as Professor, Prophet, W.F., and Wallace—to illustrate and locate these names as "mere artifacts of a particular formation."

> The Honorable Master Elijah Muhammad taught very vaguely about the Honorable Master Fard Muhammad as a person. He said that he was a "savior," he said he was "God," and he said that he was "God in the person of Master Fard Muhammad." He also said that Master Fard told him that he would have to go away and that he (the Honorable Elijah Muhammad) would have to do the job. . . . You don't need me any more.[50]

In efforts to demystify the person of Fard Muhammad, Imam Muhammad reminded the community of all the names by which his father had referred to Fard to point out that the emphasis was on the task of Honorable Elijah Muhammad. By redirecting community members to give prominence to the assignment of changing the condition of black people, Imam Muhammad was able to contextualize the history of the community and provide new direction.

> If you design a revolution to bring people out of their condition into another condition, you cannot

> continue to always put emphasis on revolution. . . . Master Fard Muhammad had a design to bring about changes that would bring us into a new world, a new life, and a new mind. . . . Now we are at the structure. . . . the Honorable Elijah Muhammad began to gradually take the emphasis off of battle strategy and put it on building. . . . Today we have arrived at our goal and the trip was successful. . . . If we get busy right now and build the new world. I assure you that we will not be ruled by any other government in the new world but our own self-government.[51]

Explaining his father's philosophy, Imam Muhammad described African Americans as creatures who indeed have souls, but whose legacy of slavery has wiped out all of their self-knowledge. African Americans were and are available to have their being written upon by anyone, in particular by their "former" masters. The position of the Nation was that sense of self had to be restored first. What also comes to light in this discussion is that Islam seats itself in already formed cultures, acting to reinterpret or redirect, and sometimes eliminate traditional values and virtues, but never to form humans. This is why Elijah Muhammad could not give the "true" Islam to his community, as presented by immigrant Muslims. Islam did not and could not take hold a generation after the legal end of slavery. It could make no sense to "empty vessels" (African Americans), who were unable to understand themselves as actors in this world. As a direct consequence, sense of self had to be reintroduced and nourished prior to any reception of the full teachings of Islam as presented by Imam Muhammad.

In Nation of Islam philosophy what African Americans were lacking, as evidenced by their taking of an assigned ethnicity and slave names, was the ability to create, to act out or even think they could control their own earthly destinies. But the ex–chattel slaves understood spirituality, and their souls were receptive to what spirituality stirred in them. Information alone was not enough to nourish a people who had been forced to transgress normal mental, spiritual, and moral boundaries. What was needed was to be fully human with a self- or group-determined identity—along with all the myths that entails—as well as homes, goals, institutions, and so on.

Now it is quite obvious that ex-slaves understood the power of money, but what was lacking was the information on how to accumulate capital and make it work for them. "The way to get these people, Elijah, is to hold out to them the bait that represents to them the things that they need and want right now."[52] These "things" were an identity; a worldview resting on faith in God, not on the inferiority or the superiority of races; and membership in a self-protected community experiencing some measure of decent living from one's own efforts. This foundation, having been articulated in the works (factories, businesses) that the Nation of Islam was able to produce, was to be the springboard into the world community of Islam. Now the community could enter the world community on its own terms as a "people" appropriating Islam, just as other Islamic communities in the world had done before them.

During this period of rapid transition under the leadership of Imam Muhammad, the Nation of Islam evolved into the World Community of Islam in the West (also called the Lost-Found Nation of Islam in the West). The emerging image and worldview of the Nation as part of the broader Islamic community was also reflected in individual name changes. In an address on the relative ineffectiveness of the civil rights movement, Imam Muhammad suggested that African Americans could really impact a new consciousness in America if they were all to legally adopt Muslim names. Members of the Nation thus began to relinquish their Xs in favor of more traditional Muslim names.

Imam Muhammad then suggested to the community that a more fitting name for them could be found in the person of a major person of African heritage in the history of early Islam,

Bilal Ibn Ribah. Bilal Ibn Ribah was a companion of the Prophet Muhammad, and an Abyssinian slave who converted to Islam and became one of the most respected military leaders under the Prophet. Of Bilal, Imam Muhammad wrote:

> We believe that the term "Bilal" identifies us with a person in history. We know that the name Bilal itself really refers to the soul; and Bilal was a person who was highly spiritual. . . . So this inner sensitivity is what we identify with in Bilal.[53]

Although identification with this figure did not lead to a generally accepted name-change in the movement, it did instigate a change in the name of the Nation's newspaper, as *Muhammad Speaks* became the *Bilalian News.*

During this time the Muslim-Christian Dialogue Program was also initiated. In this program Imams and their community members went out in their locales to visit accommodating Christian churches and synagogues to engage in conversations over representations of the Divine. This program often resulted in lively debates held over several months. The other major program carried out at this time was the more traditional *dawah* program. In this program, community members (men primarily) went to homes of non-Muslims to talk about Islam, sold *Bilalian News*, and handed out flyers consisting of excerpts from the lectures of Imam Mohammed in neighborhoods and on college campuses. The community was also able to give away copies of the Yusef Ali translation of the *Qur'an*, which had been donated to them by Saudi Arabia via the Muslim Student's Association for such purposes.

The Muslim-Christian Dialogue Program and the *dawah* program were fueled by C.R.A.I.D. (The Committee to Remove All Images that Attempt to Portray the Divine), founded in 1977. This committee secured space in the community's newspaper to run a weekly article. C.R.A.I.D.'s attention was focused on the elimination of pictures portraying a white Jesus. Another aim of the organization was to collect ten million signatures on petitions to "request that Imam Warith Deen Mohammed and Pope John Paul II meet and share with the public their views on racial divinities in religion."[54]

Simultaneously, the community invested in carrying on the legacy of religious education built in the Nation of Islam. All the University of Islam schools were renamed the Clara Muhammad School after the school in Chicago. Classes continued to be gender-segregated. Curricula were extended and young Muslims were graduating and entering some of the best colleges and universities in America, proving that knowledge of self coupled with a good foundation in basic education was one road to success. Continuing the push to confront the primacy of images of the Divine and the racial divinities issues in America, members of the World Community of Islam in the West at once maintained the integrity of the community while reaching out and establishing linkages with others. Publication of the *World Muslim News* in the beginning of the 1980s signaled another opening up of this community to the world and the further building of connections to other Muslims. The brief duration of this publication does not speak to its significant influence (both home and abroad).

As the parameters of the relationship between this community and the world community of Muslims became clearer, the World Community of Islam in the West appeared to feel more confident in its place. This confidence was heralded by the adoption of the name of the American Muslim Mission for the community and the title *AM Journal* for the newspaper in 1982. By 1984 the various communities were no longer centrally bound in any obvious way. Local imams had autonomy to guide their communities as they chose, although they never really exercised it, remaining committed to the leadership of Imam Muhammad and his guidance in reading and understanding the *Qur'an.*

In recent years, Imam Mohammed has taken an increasingly international position in response to world events, while simultaneously encouraging those community imams who follow his leadership to improve their Islamic knowledge and take civic leadership.

He has made sizable contributions to both American and Muslim charities. It is noteworthy, however, that the tension between nation-building and *ummah* is escalating, as the needs for community resources increase and Muslim world crises ebb and flow. The loss of the framework (busineses and property) built by Elijah Muhammad when the Nation was at its peak has also necessitated a rebuilding.

The Nation of Islam: Louis Farrakhan

> I, Louis Farrakhan, am saying to the world that the Honorable Elijah Muhammad is not physically dead. I am further stating that he was made to appear as such as written in the Bible and in the Holy Qur'an, in order that the Holy Qur'an, in order that the Scriptures might be fulfilled.[55]

> The Honorable Elijah Muhammad is the man that taught me what I know, and he is the man that gave me an example to pattern my life after. I respect and love him immensely. There is nothing that anybody can say to me that will make me put him down or discredit him. That man did what nobody else has done. The problem is, we can't stay where we were. We have to move on.[56]

> The very thought that we would associate a rival or partner with Allah (God) positions us as a loser. Our loved ones cannot save us. Our powerful leaders whom we admire cannot save us. There is no refuge today in

> anyone but in Allah, the Almighty God. And when we seek refuge in Him, and put our trust completely in Him, then and only then will we be able to say that we are one of the overcomers.[57]

In an apparent difference of opinion on the direction of the World Community of Islam in the West, Minister Louis Farrakhan, after the death of the Honorable Elijah Muhammad, left the community to reestablish the Nation of Islam. This obvious move away from *ummah* and back to *'asabiya* proved to involve a long legal struggle. Through this struggle Minister Farrakhan succeeded in acquiring the major temple and the residence of Elijah Muhammad in Chicago. The temple was renamed Mosque Maryam and Muhammad's University of Islam School was reopened. All of the other schools, restaurants, bakeries, garment shops, and so on were closed, and properties were sold by Imam Wallace Muhammad to pay legal fees.[58] The tensions caused by the legal battles between W. D. Muhammad and the other children of the Honorable Elijah Muhammad are a subject in themselves that will not be discussed here. The Islamic growth in this community is what we will explore.

The *Final Call* newspaper along with public lectures by the Honorable Louis Farrakhan and his ministers are a good barometer of Islamic growth. This Nation of Islam has chosen to keep its focus primarily on educating African Americans and other minorities with regard to their struggle in a racist society. This goal has been augmented by cementing alliances with African Muslims. Mumar al-Ghaddafi's five-million-dollar interest-free loan in the 1980s to the Nation of Islam to support the rebuilding of businesses was the first of these alliances.

The community continues to assert, without alteration, the *Muslim Program.* As in the first half of the century, the *Final Call* carries on the back page a statement of purpose entitled "*What the Muslims Believe.*" The statement includes the following.

1. We believe in the One God whose proper name is Allah.
2. We believe in the Holy Qur'an and in the Scriptures of all the Prophets of God.
3. We believe in the truth of the Bible, but we believe that it has been tampered with and must be reinterpreted so that mankind will not be snared by the falsehoods that have been added to it.
4. We believe in Allah's Prophets and the Scriptures they brought to the people.
5. We believe in the resurrection of the dead—not in physical resurrection—but in mental resurrection. . . .
6. We believe in the judgement; we believe this first judgement will take place as God revealed, in America. . . .
7. We believe this is time in history for the separation of the so-called Negroes and the so-called white Americans. . . .
8. We believe in justice for all. . . .
9. We believe that the offer of integration is hypocritical. . . .
10. We believe that we who declare ourselves to be righteous Muslims, should not participate in wars which take the lives of humans. . . .
11. We believe our women should be respected and protected as the women of other nationalities are respected and protected.
12. We believe that Allah (God) appeared in the person of Master

> W. Fard Muhammad, July, 1930; the long-awaited "Messiah" of the Christians and the "Mahdi" of the Muslims. We believe further and lastly that Allah is God and besides Him there is no God and he will bring about a universal government of peace wherein we all can live in peace together.

In accordance with these beliefs, the ministers in the Nation use both the Bible and the *Qur'an.* In recent years, as contact increases with African Muslims, ministers are being trained in Islamic studies, and shaykhs are being brought in to teach the use of Arabic and *ayat* (the smallest unit of recitation) from the *Qur'an.* Slowly but surely the Nation of Islam is cautiously embracing Islamic obligations, though it is still extremely cautious about embracing the Muslim world. As in some other communities, this community also judges the Muslim world by its actions.

The community continues its uses of what is now called the "December Fast" to distinguish it from Ramadan. This fast serves the purpose of promoting self-discipline and restraint on the part of the members of the community during the Christian holiday season. Many members of the community participate in Ramadan as well, and with Minister Farrakhan's urging (not order) the number increases yearly. With regard to other core Islamic obligations, such as new members' establishing a *shahadah*, paying *zakat*, or making the *hajj*, there is no evidence that the community as a whole has had instruction in these areas. It is known, however, that some members claim to do all of the core obligations. The sending in of the letter to receive an X is still practiced, but now new members receive an Arabic name. The original texts of Maulana Ali—the *Holy Qur'an* and commentary, along with *The Religion of Islam* and prayer books—have been reprinted and are readily available in all of the Nation's bookstores. My assumption is that some members are studying them and do practice the core Islamic obligations.

Since 1984 and the concrete reemergence of the Nation of Islam, there have been numerous confrontations with issues from the past. Among these issues are the involvement of the Nation in the death of Malcolm X and the stories surrounding the Honorable Elijah Muhammad's personal life. Minister Farrakhan has addressed both these particular issues in his Saviour's Day 1993 lecture, which he dedicated to Sister Clara Muhammad, Elijah Muhammad's later wives, the family of Malcolm X, Spike Lee, and the Honorable Elijah Muhammad.

> At the center of the controversy is the domestic life of the Hon. Elijah Muhammad, who was referred to by his followers as the Messenger of Allah, and whether that aspect of the controversy caused the Messenger to order the murder of Malcom X.
>
> But the Hon. Elijah Muhammad never ordered anyone to kill Malcom X, he said.[59]

The general assertion by members of the Nation of Islam with regard to the murder of Malcolm X is that he was murdered by CIA and FBI infiltrators. This assertion has been made candidly, as has the statement that any Muslim would have been prepared to kill Malcolm X, because he had defamed his teacher. Several participants in the Saviours' Day meeting hailed these assertions as the first step in healing.

Sister Tynetta Muhammad, a one-time secretary and former wife of Elijah Muhammad, has assumed the role of "mother" of the believers. Clara Muhammad, the first wife of Elijah Muhammad, is now rarely mentioned in the community. Her son Ishmail and the son of another of the Elijah Muhammad's wives have been ministers in training. These men are highly respected in the community, and are expected to succeed Minister Farrakhan by some members.

The Nation of Islam, since its full-fledged reemergence in 1984, has been involved in a number of significant projects with respect to the general African American community. It has, through the efforts of Dr. Abdul Alim Muhammad and Dr. Barbara Justice, worked diligently with AIDS patients and the licensing of new therapy. Even though these efforts have been maligned and fought by the general medical community, the medical team persists with the support of the African American community. The Nation has also organized a successful security business called N.O.I. Security to police neighborhoods in high-crime areas in several major cities. The success of this operation has made national news.

The Nation of Islam: Minister John Muhammad

Just as Farrakhan found the World Community of Islam in the West problematic, so to did Minister John Muhammad, the Honorable Elijah Muhammad's brother. From his Temple in Highland Park, Michigan, Minister John Muhammad, Supreme Minister of the Nation of Islam continues his interpretation of what his brother designed for black people living in America. He has restored Muhammad University of Islam, along with the temple (although not on the original site) which had been demolished long ago. Members of this community use both the *Holy Qur'an* by Maulana Yusuf Ali and the Holy Bible for guidance. The name of their newspaper is *Muhammad Speaks Continues*, which uses a number of quotes from the original *Muhammad Speaks*, as well as the texts of the Honorable Elijah Muhammad. Interestingly, we had a great deal of difficulty finding the temple. While members of Minister Farrakhan's Nation were out selling papers, there was no clue in the community that this place existed. When two other researchers and I tried to visit the community temple we were told that Minister Muhammad spoke every Sunday and the public was invited.

To distinguish what they believe from the beliefs of Farrakhan's community, followers of Minister Muhammad offer a statement printed on the last page of their newspaper. This statement of belief asserts:

> We Believe
> Allah came in the Person of Master Fard Muhammad.
> We Believe
> The Honorable Elijah Muhammad was the Last Messenger of Allah.
> We Believe
> Messenger Elijah Muhammad died a physical death February 25, 1975 and will not return.
> We Believe
> The Honorable John Muhammad is the Supreme Minister of the Nation of Islam.
> We believe
> The White man is, was and always will be, the Real Devil.

Members of this community still uphold the December Fast as a total fast from food, drink, marital relations, and so on, from sunrise to sunset. What is Islam? Islam is wisdom. Islam is guidance of God for man. Islam is the only way of God. What is a Muslim?

> As I have foresaid, Allah (God) in the Person of Master Fard Muhammad, to Whom Praises are due forever, has taught me that all Black men, Black women and Black children are Muslim, by nature. [60]

In community practice there is no mention made of a *shahadah*, *salat*, *zakat*, or *hajj*. Believers are encouraged to pray and to invite black people to the temple so that they can get on the road out of poverty and misery.

Darul Islam under Imam Jamil Al-Amin

> The mission of a believer in Islam is totally different from coexisting or being a part of the system. The prevailing morals are wrong. [Modern] Western philosophy . . . has reduced man to food, clothing, shelter, and the sex drive, which means he doesn't have a spirit. In Islam, we're not talking about empowering people with money. We're talking about overturning that whole thing, man. [61]

There are at least thirty communites in the United States and the Caribbean who have pledged their allegiance to Imam Jamil Al-Amin. Imam Jamil's response to why he moved into Islam is an articulation commonly expressed by Muslims who have been active in the black power movement.

> See, most people don't have a true picture of what Islam is. Islam is not non-violent. There is right to self-defense, and there is right to defend your faith. Allah says that fighting is prescribed for you. . . . [62]

> It became even evident that to accomplish the things we had talked about in the struggle, you would need a practice. Allah says He does not change the condition of people until they change that which is in themselves. That is what Islam does, and it points out right from wrong. It points out truth from falsehood. [63]

Focusing on *salat* as the organizing principle, a philosophy for the discipline necessary to effect Islam is built.

> ALLAH establishes a practice that man can copy; we can do what other humans do, we can emulate what men do. If we look at historical acts of the Prophet and his companions, we see a clear blueprint for changing a society, for bringing about revolutionary change even under the most difficult conditions.[64]

In *Revolution by the Book*, Imam Jamil elaborates the organization of community focusing on principles such as *zakat. Zakat* is defined as "to spend from that which we have as our means of purifying that which we keep." Contributing to the understanding of the community, *zakat* teaches Muslims about sacrifice, and how to use community resources to generate an economy—"to barter and trade, amongs ourselves."[65] *Sadaqa* (charity) and *zakat* work hand in hand to clarify the importance of self-restraint in the growth of the Muslim personality. Successful social struggle must have as a part of its foundation an actively implemented understanding of charity. The welfare of the Muslim community cannot be dependent on a non-Muslim society.

Sawm (fasting) is another form of the discipline necessary to both bind the community and teach the Muslim how "to guard against evil." The object of sawm is "to gain God-consciouness."[66] The Muslim must on an ongoing basis abstain from those foods and drinks that are not good for the body. Imam Jamil specifically targets the multitude of artificial ingredients in some powdered drinks and food stuffs that are pushed by the media for consumption. Fasting from food is not the only aspect of fasting. Fasting from the intake of misleading and/or corrupt information is also necessary. Along these lines, Muslims in these communities strive to control the information introduced into their households through the various kinds of media—television, radio, magazines, and so on.

In the revolution that occurs when one becomes Muslim, the need for an ethnic identity is vital, but is not sufficient.

> You have to go beyond the whole concept of nationalism when you are talking about successful struggle. . . . So, race becomes something that is insignificant when you try to trace it all the way back; because you can't go any further than Adam. [67]

> Peoplehood is based upon belief more than anything else. More than race, more than on any psychological characteristics, peoplehood is determined by belief; Allah has given us many narratives in the Qur'an than can substitute this.[68]

Upholding the Islamic understanding of social justice, Imam Jamil's communities look to the *Qur'an* for an accurate account of oppression, and for guidance in resolving the problem.

> And what reason have you that you should not fight in the way of Allah, and of those who, being weak, are ill-treated and (oppressed)? Men, women and children, whose cry is: "Our Lord! rescue us from this town whose people are oppressors, and raise for us from Thee one who will protect; and raise for us from Thee one who will help."[69]

In reflection on the struggle of African Americans against racism, this philosophy asserts that the struggle has been waged without having a firm foundation that reforms the character of the individual toward traits necessary for success. As a *Qur'an*-based community which is using the first Muslim community as the example, there is a focus on establishing belief and the principles which will lay the foundation for education and self-sufficiency.

In conversations with community members, several themes emerge that warrant mentioning: an emphasis first, on the notion of character reformation, second, on a consistency of Islamic practice by members; and third on the idea of a nurturing community to support those who err. Lastly, each community member that I spoke with asserted that their local community definitely had ties with the other communities, all of which followed a set of basic principles. They did not feel that they were in competition with other communities, and often worked with them on social events.

"Sufi" Communities[70]

The word "sufi" refers to a person who is initiated in the "way to God." Sufis have found the way to God in allegorical and symbolic interpretations of the *Qur'an* and the life of the Prophet Muhammad. The "way" of Muslims is most often described as the *Shari'ah* (Divine Law) which orders the life of the community while the *Tariqa* (way to God) elaborates a method for individual spirituality under the guidance of a shaykh and specifically a type of Sufi order. The place of this method for spirituality in relationship to the law has for centuries caused dissonance, primarily because of its potential to overshadow the law. The first well-established evidence of sufism as a movement dates from the tenth century, with organized associations of sufis with lineages and influence appearing in the eleventh century. At the heart of the diverse practices of the various orders is the *dhikr*. The term *dhikr* (a remembrance, reminder, commemoration) is used in the *Qur'an* with reference to God more than fifty times.

> O Ye who believe! Celebrate the praises of God And do this often. (33:41)
>
> Surely this [the Revelation] is a Reminder; so let him who will, take unto his Lord a way. (73:19; 76:29)
>
> Islam is spoken of in general throughout the Qur'an as "the way of God," that is, the path ordained by god, which may be said to include both esoterism and exoterism. But "the way of God" mentioned only in these two *sunnan* (above) is clearly the esoteric path, and the causality here is strengthened by the word "Reminder" —that which produces rememberance (*dhikr*), which is itself the essence of Sufism.[71]

Remembering God; the Remembrance (the *Qur'an*); the Revelation as Reminder as "the Way to God" are at once in the essence of Islam and an added spiritual dimension in Islam. The Arabic term for a remembrance, reminder is *dhikr.* In everyday Islam, remembering God is at the center of belief and practice—especially formal prayers five times daily. After each of these prayers most Muslims spend a few extra moments in a *dhikr*—the repetition of *Subhan Allah*, *Al-Hamdu li'llah*, and *Allahu Akbar*, each repeated thirty-three times counted out on fingers or *dhikr* beads. For some Muslims, since the days of Prophet Muhammad there has been an inclination to pursue "the way to God" in an even more ritualized, disciplined fashion which I call the "added dimension," or, more specifically "the Way."

"The Way" or *tariqa* evolved over time from an individual assertion to a group assertion under the guidance of masters called shaykhs. These shaykhs are understood to possess special knowledge as a result of arduous spiritual *jihads* (struggles). The eleventh and twelfth centuries are filled with accounts of masters who draw large numbers of students to their guidance. "The way" does not differentiate itself from everyday Islamic practice, and as a result travelling shaykhs spread their "way" and Islam to various populations. *Turuq* (plural of *tariqa*) are organized around different stages (maqaamaat) that lead to God.

The history of *tariqa* includes the accounts of masters who sought total union with God and those who used the discipline and the *dhikr* to discover and act upon God's will. While each *tariqa* has a unique *dhikr* and set of ritual observances, there is a common framework. The basic relationship is between shaykh and student. Students are initiated to the path; memorize the lineage (ancestry) of the group; memorize the *dhikr* and learn prayers that assist them along the path. Students seek to rid themselves of self-centeredness. This is done by a progressive process under the guidance of the shaykh. Getting control over desires such as accumulation of material wealth and selfishness is achieved by degrees. As the student moves along the path his/her ability to understand God's will and act upon it improve in direct proportion to the dedication in practicing the *dhikr*.

The *tariqa* is composed of male and female students.

> It is in fact miraculous that a period of fourteen centuries with all of its trials and confrontations could not break the continuity in beliefs, thoughts, and actions between the women who are blessed with the company of the Prophet and led a spiritual life under his guidance (*sahabiyat*) in the beginning of the Islamic era. . . .
>
> The women who followed the teachings of Qur'an, like their Muslim male counterparts, strove to model their behavior on the example set by

> the Prophet, his companions, and his household.[72]

Sufism acknowledges that "no distinction can be made between Muslim men and women on their capacity and longing to reach the divine." Sufism has provided a realm where women's sprituality can be nurtured throughout the history of Islam. There are *muqadamah* (female teachers) and *shaykhat* (female guides). Women are seen as having the potential to practice Islam directly. While opening up spiritual pathways, *tariqa* have also been active in the assertion of Islam against its enemies. Leaders and students of *tariqas* have been in the forefront of movements against colonial powers in the Muslim world. Just as most Islamic expressions in the world have come to the United States, so have at least two major *tariqas*—the *Nayshabandiyyah*, and *Tjaniyyah.*

Naqshabandiyyah

This name and initial affiliation come from Khwajah Baha al-Din Muhammad Naqshaband (1317–1389 A.D.). Naqshabandiyyah was established in central Asia before expanding to Turkey, Afghanistan, Syria, India and finally today to the United States. This *tariqa*, which became a movement in the United States in 1986, is fast growing and attracting numbers of African Americans. There are at least five *muqadam* (teachers) in the U.S. with *dhikr* circles in almost every major urban city. Recently the *tariqa* purchased 180 acres in Fenton, Michigan as a *zawiya* for everyone (any faith) searching to improve their spirituality. The current shaykh (fortieth in line) is Maulan Shaykh Nazim Adil Qubrusi from Turkey. To this date there are Naqshabandi in seventy-three countries who represent their affiliation by the colors of the turbans worn by men—Britain (blue), Germany (purple), Pakistan (black), Hispanics (gold), African American (red). African Americans wear red, according to Rashid Hassan, the *muqadam* in Chicago,

> because African Americans are very spiritually powerful and also because

> Shaykh Nazim says that African-Americans are very spiritually powerful and also because the Mahdi awaited by Muslims will be of African Descent and will be wearing a red turban—he will be of the line of Prophet Muhammad. African Americans are the vanguard.[73]

Spiritual connectedness is traced from Allah to Prophet Muhammad to Abu Bakr (the successor to Prophet Muhammad). The *tariqa* is a spiritual path to Allah. "One can not reach *tariqa* except through Shari'ah and Sunnah. If one sees this as a journey, the community of believers are on the ship of Shari'ah guided by the shaykh (the possessor of *mari'fa*—divine knowledge)." Divine order is always sent to guide through the person of the shaykh—to bring the believer to Allah. A person may have information which he/she can attempt to interpret, but gains knowledge and spiritual power from the shaykh. While believing that "there are no more Books or Prophets, Naqshabandi assert that "revelations are still unfolding." Students of the Shaykh seek to reach their "spiritual destinations" through recognition of their negative aspects; understanding that spirituality is transferred from heart to heart—from shaykh to student; submitting their will to the unseen; and above all comprehending that they must be guided back to the Creator—through the Prophet Muhammad. Each person is accountable for his/her actions—"God does not need you, you need Him." The physical Shari'ah and Sunnah teach what is lawful and unlawful—right and wrong with regard to *adab* (everyday etiquette), and the Muslim must follow these rules of conduct.

Dhikr circles are held twice weekly to embrace the spiritual power in congregation and to experience Divine knowledge, which cannot be reached through the intellect. There is a preference for *Jum'ah* prayer to be held in the company of other Naqshabandi, although students do visit other communites frequently for dialogue and to "engage hearts." One source of confusion, asserts

Rashid Hassan, is that

> people do not believe that Prophets are still living. Muhammad is the beloved one, the last Prophet and the first Light. We can not approach Allah except through Prophet Muhammad—Prophet Muhammad is not out of existence—spirituality is transferred heart to heart. Allah is sending His friends to guide and does so through a *sadiq* (one who is trustworthy).

Currently there are about one-thousand students in the Naqshabadiyya movement.

Tijaniyyah

Abu'l-'Abbas ben Muhammad ben al-Mukhtar at-Tijani (born in 1737 in the south of Algeria) asserted that he received permission from Prophet Muhammad to teach the Way. By the nineteenth century this *tariqa* had become a serious political force south of the Sahara as they played a critical role in the resistance to French occupation and colonial domination. Tijaniyyah came to New York with Ahmad Dempson (a Ghanaian) in 1970. This *muqadam* was a student of Shaykh Muhammad Sani Aswal of Nigeria, who was a close companion of the Grand Imam Shaykh Ibrahim Niasse of Kaolak.

Here in the United States the most popular Shaykh is Shaykh Hassan Cisse, grandson of Ibrahim ibn Abdullah Niasse. Shaykh Cisse has initiated and authorized a number of African American *muqadam* along the eastern seaboard and some in the Midwest. The growth and dedication of this *tariqa* is most evident in the ties forged with the *tariqa* in Senegal. There is at least one predominately African American *madrasah* (*Qur'an* school) in Senegal funded by the *tariqa* in the United States.

Tijanis are "strict about performing the five prayers in congregation and in observing the legal obligations."[74] One focus here is on virtues and moving toward selflessness. Students seek to improve their spiritual lives by working on personal deficits. In some communities members gather several times weekly at the home of a *muqadam* or *muqadamah* for the *dhikr*. Estimates of participants in this *tariqa* number around two-thousand.

3 The Family Structure and Domestic Life

تلك حدود الله ومن يطع الله ورسوله يدخله
جنت تجري من تحتها الانهر خلدين فيها و
ذلك الفوز العظيم ﴿١٣﴾

These are Allah's limits; and whosoever obeys Allah and His Apostle, He will cause him to enter gardens beneath which rivers flow, to abide in them; and this is the great achievement.

—Sura Nisa 4:13.

THIS CHAPTER WILL focus on contemporary family life in African American Islamic communities by examining the topics of marriage, divorce, childrearing, gender relations, and death and funeral rites. Previous chapters have shown that there is considerable diversity in African- American Islam, and we can expect that this diversity will be reflected in family life. The principal determinants of family life are soci–economic status and Islamic understandings—e.g., those focusing on nation-building versus *ummah.* Since these factors are constantly evolving both within communities and amongst individuals, changes in family life will occur. The reader is therefore cautioned against interpreting the examples discussed in this chapter as if they were cast in stone.

THE INSTITUTION OF MARRIAGE

Primarily because the *Qur'an* urges marriage and prohibits casual gender mixing, marriage is understood within African American Muslim communities as protection and a secure status. The general criteria for marriage include being of sound mind and body and being actively religious (i.e., praying daily, fasting during Ramadan, paying *zakat*, and so on). Men are also expected to have some means of earning a living with which to support a family and, preferably, some savings. Beyond these core criteria, there are other expectations. In many communities, there is the expectation that spouses will be chosen from within the community. In other communities, spouses are chosen from the larger community of Muslims, which includes immigrants. There is a general understanding that Muslim women can only marry Muslim men. In most communities when Muslim women want to marry wen who are not Muslim (a rarity), the men in question are generally also accepting of Islam. Muslim men have the choice of marrying believing women from among the Christian and Jewish communities, but do not exercise this right to any great extent in the communities I have explored.

Women have an easy or difficult time finding a husband depending on their economic status, educational status, and/or previous marriage record. In general, women who have never married and have no children are considered ideal marriage prospects. Women who are well educated and in highly visible career positions are often not viewed so favorably, since men tend to regard the professional commitments of these women as problematic. Thus, even though the male population is much larger, in many communities there tends to be high a percentage of unmarried, educated women. Divorced women, especially those with children, are also not considered ideal marriage prospects. Women in this category generally are required to make financial provisions for their children separate from any prospective marriage. Muslim men are especially reticent to take on the role of guardian to teenage children from a potential spouse's previous marriage.

Men and women both tend to follow the Islamic criteria for seeking mates. What the members of a community have to say about the character and integrity of prospective spouses weighs a great deal in the choices of mates. Inside communities, men and women who are pious and hardworking are generally well known. In older, well-established communities, such as the Moorish Science Temple and the Nation of Islam, families have had the chance to see children grow up, observe who has been divorced, and so on, and their ability to see potential marriage arrangements is therefore good. In communities with high turnover of members, this ability diminshes proportionately. In some communities, serious efforts are made to determine the character of unknown Muslims who become new members. That persons who become Muslims can hide their histories is a well-known fact, and while community members accept them as part of the group, it is not often that they will give their daughters' hand in marriage.

The Premarital Period

As one might expect, premarital contact between the sexes differs significantly in African American Muslim communities as compared to non-Muslim communities. Dating in the contemporary American context is not always linked to marriage, and most often involves some degree of sexual contact. African American Muslims find this practice in direct conflict with Islamic ethics, and such dating is thus replaced by a number of alternatives. For example, there are supervised gatherings, where both young and older adults convene with the expressed purpose of meeting a potential spouse. Further supervised meetings and conversations can be arranged between prospective spouses, but the expectation is that "getting to know" someone at this stage does not involve sexual contact.

In recent decades African American Muslims, following the lead of immigrant Muslims, have taken to operating marriage services. Advertisements by singles are placed in special "matrimonial" sections in Muslim magazines and journals. Typical advertisements read:

> African American Muslim, 48, never married, seeks matrimonial correspondence from practicing Muslima with children under 10 years of age.
>
> African American computer professional, 43, divorced, one dependent, educated, seeks correspondence from educated, open-minded and family oriented, African American Muslima, over 30, children ok. Photo/Details.
>
> African American Muslima, 34, youthful, attractive, fit, 5'6", 128 lbs., sincere, loving, committed, educated, never married, seeks sincere, kind, committed, educated (master's/Ph.D.), broadminded yet believing Muslim, 30–41, prefer from Sudan or Africa. Photo/Details.[1]

Muslims who do not patronize the "matrimonials" sections of the various magazines tend to rely upon either "word of mouth" or various singles socials arranged by some masajid. Word of mouth has its pros and cons also. Often, married women or men will recommend a family friend to a single woman. In these cases, the unmarried woman has a greater chance of learning more about a potential mate, since she can ask questions about his demeanor and habits from friends who will usually give accurate information. Muslims in each community have an unspoken pact to not speak ill of one another, but generally will divulge critical information when it comes to marriage. There is also the sense that because the recommendation came from friends, there is some responsibility attached to it.

There are several points to note in regard to the proposal and engagement period. The first concerns how much personal information is exchanged by prospective spouses. On the one hand,

Islamically, there is a limit placed on the personal information divulged at this point, because the *niyyah* (intention) for marriage needs to be revealed before too much is made known about a person that is not protected by at least an oral contract. On the other hand, in the West, where communities are generally not old enough for most of the singles to be very well known, this sort of personal information is crucial before a *niyyah* is made. This dilemma continues to persist, and most African American Muslims seek to find compromises between traditional Islamic practice and the experience of life in their own common house.

When women have definitely decided that they want to become "engaged," the need for a *wali* arises. A *wali*, by dictionary definition, is "one [male] who is near to [friend of]; [a] legal guardian who has been assigned the authority to administer another's affairs."[2] Women who choose to have a *wali* most often choose the husband of a close friend in the absence of a Muslim male relative. The wali then either seeks out men for marriage or investigates already identified men. The *wali* will continue to act as an intermediary until marriage, and may even perform the marriage, thus ending his obligations in this position.

Once a proposal of marriage is made and accepted, a public announcement is usually made at the masjid. This changes the social status of the individuals and prevents others from proposing to either one of them. It also marks the beginning of a time-period during which the immediate dowry (*mahr*) is to be obtained by the man for the woman. The composition of the dowry varies widely in the Muslim world. In some communities, the dowry may be a new *Qur'an*, while in others it may be a combination of things that the woman feels she wants to own. The only thing that most African American Muslims can agree upon is that dowries are necessary for marriage.

It is at this time that the couple makes very serious efforts to get to know one another. They visit each other's families, and go out with married Muslims or relatives so that they can spend some time with each other purposefully—i.e., planning for marriage and discussing issues such as children and housing. During this time, the terms of the marriage contract are spelled out. In the contract, the when, where, and whys are elaborated. Points to be discussed might include: whether a wife will continue her studies, or career, whether polygyny will be permitted. Marriage contracts can be renegotiated at any time, but must be agreed to prior to the actual wedding. A wedding date is set and friends and family notified.

There are exceptions to this scenario in some communities and under certain circumstances. For example, if prospective spouses are estranged from their families, the proposal and marriage process become community-centered affairs. In such situations, very little planning occurs and the proposal and marriage take place sometimes within days to avoid sexual temptation.

Some *masajid* have developed Islamic marriage-license forms that are filled out before, at, or shortly after the wedding. In these communities, a copy of the form is kept on file in the masajid and the couple keep the original. Some communities require a civil license before the Islamic marriage license is issued. The possibilities for future problems when just an Islamic marriage license is issued are great. Various states recognize Islamic marriage as either "common-law" unions or "religious" unions and the couple receive rights and privileges accordingly. Problems arise in cases of divorce and polygyny, which will be discussed later in this chapter.

Although most African American Muslims opt for Islamic marriages, some choose to get married outside of the community. Such persons usually get married in a private home with the proper number of witnesses (two males) present. Although this type of marriage is actively discouraged, it happens. In these cases, a dowery is still needed, and a marriage contract is also a necessity. It is important to note, however, that in many communities women have not taken advantage of the Qur'anic requirement for a marriage contract.

Weddings

Wedding preparations (in communities that have formal weddings) are generally Western, except for a few things "Islamic." There are no bridesmaids, flower girls, ring bearers, or walks down an aisle. There is, however, a swell of activity revolving around food preparation, getting a wedding dress made, arranging for a wedding site, getting invitations in the mail. Family, Muslim and non-Muslim, participate in the preparation in most communities. Recently, some couples have begun to arrange for formal pictures and/or videotapes of the wedding. Lambs are slaughtered, loads of fresh fruit are brought in, and the *masjid* or hall is decorated. There is no music, but this does not detract from the festive air.

Men are separated from women, in most communities, from the beginning to the end of the ceremony, as they generally are in most social events. The reception is held directly afterward and gifts are given to the couple. The couple is not detained long at the reception. After a few hours, they gather their gifts and go home or to an undisclosed destination to begin a three-day period of uninterrupted privacy. No one will seek to disturb the couple during this time unless there is an emergency. The couple comes out in public after this period is over.

Polygyny

There are many questions concerning the practice of polygyny in African American Muslim communities, and all of them can not be answered here. Perhaps the most asked question is: How can American women ever consider such a practice? It is important to note that polygyny is not the norm across these communities, though at particular points in the contemporary era it has been a statistically significant form of marriage in the Darul Islam, Islamic Party, and Ansarullah communities. It is also present in the communities of Imam Warithudeen (Wallace C. Muhammad and others) but not significantly. In any community, when the leadership becomes involved in polygynous relationships, the practice becomes viewed as a viable alternative for a time in that community. Some men interviewed say that "the women who are single need the protection and security of marriage and there are few eligible men." There are women who agree with this assertion and add that "once Muslim, a woman's social life is mostly restricted to the community and the number of working, responsible men is low." Women also assert that "there are real economic and security issues for Muslim women that keeps the notion of polygyny alive."[3] The actual number of polygynous relationships is unavailable.

The issues surrounding polygyny as a viable alternative to monogamy are also multiple and complex. First, there are issues that focus on the validity of marriage itself. Marriage in Islam is a public event (in varying degrees), and is meant to legally bind men and women to determine parentage of children, along with inheritance rights and other obligations. This creates a source of conflicts because, on one hand, to make polygyny public would be problematic in America (American law in most states makes any form of polygyny illegal), while, on the other hand, secretive marriages deprive women of their Islamic rights. Another issue is economic, and concerns the difficulty of maintaining two or more households. Very few men are capable of supporting more than one household, and in many cases women in polygynous relationships must financially support themselves, thus negating one of the asserted reasons for the marriage. Problems also arise in regard to sharing time with various wives and family.

Divorce

Divorce in Islam is strongly discouraged, although it is permitted. When consultation does not resolve serious marriage difficulties, the *Qur'an* says:

> Those who vow (to abstain) from their wives, (the maximum) period of waiting (for them) is four months (after which divorce becomes inevitable), then if they (are reconciled within four months and) revert (to their normal relations), then surely, Allah is the Great Protector, Ever Merciful. (2:226)

But if they have resolved on divorce, then (they should know that) surely Allah is All-Hearing, All-Knowing. (2:227)

And the divorced women must keep themselves waiting for three (monthly) courses (as Iddat), and it is not lawful for them to conceal what Allah has created in their wombs, if indeed they believe in Allah and the Last Day. And their husbands have a better right to take them back in the meanwhile, provided they desire and mean reconciliation. And women have their rights similar to their obligations in an equitable and just manner; yet men have a place above them. And Allah is All-Mighty, All-Wise. (2:228)

Such a (revocable) divorce may be (pronounced) twice, then (after second pronouncement) there should be either retaining (the wife) with honor and fairness or letting (her) leave with goodness. And it is not lawful for you to take (back) anything of what you have given them (your wives); however, if both (the husband and the wife) fear that they cannot abide by the injunctions of Allah, and if you (also) fear that they cannot observe the limits (prescribed) by Allah then there is no blame on either of them in what she gives up to redeem herself (as *Khula*). These are the injunctions of Allah, therefore, do not violate them; and whoso violates the injunctions of Allah, it is they who are really wrongdoers. (2:229)

The *Qur'an* continues with guidance for some of the possibilities of relationships involving divorce. For instance, as long as a woman has not been divorced three consecutive times, she may remarry her husband. If the third divorce by the husband has happened, then she must remarry and be divorced before she may marry the former husband again. If she is pregnant when the divorce occurs, the divorce is not final until the birth of the child, and the husband is responsible for her maintenance during this period.

The procedure for divorce in the general African American Muslim community depends first on how the couple was married. If the marriage was an Islamic marriage only, the couple is usually first encouraged to seek counseling, often with witnesses from both sides to corroborate their testimony (the presence of witnesses is called for in the *Qur'an*). The counseling sessions in most communities usually involve a couple and a male (usually the Imam) respected by both parties, who acts to hear both sides of the problem/situation, and to assist, if possible, in effecting a reconciliation.

Generally, there is no public announcement of the divorce; word travels instead by conversation. The wife spends the three months of waiting sometimes with support from the husband, sometimes without support, regardless of whether or not there are children. In some situations, if the financial foundations of the home depended on the income of the husband alone, the wife seeks public assistance until she can find employment or can make her needs known to the community at large and receive *sadaqa* (charity).

Children generally stay with the mother (with the exception of the Ansarullah community), and become her responsibility until they marry or otherwise leave home. The divorce rate has not been measured with respect to the African American Muslim community, or the general American Muslim community.

In marriages where there is both an Islamic marriage and a civil marriage, all of the sanctions of United States law are active. The Islamic divorce proceeds as described previously, and then the couple follow civil procedures for divorce and any dissolution of property. Alimony and child support are subject to the state courts.

THE HOME AS A SPACE OF CULTURE FORMATION

Although we typically understand space as "a physical expanse in which objects exist and move,"[4] humans tend to *use* and *conceptualize* space in a variety of ways. Uses and concepts of space, we know, have different meanings across cultures, including notions of public, private, and sacred space that are architecturally distinct. Muslims have blended their ongoing notions of space into the specific needs of Islam—i.e., to the principles and practices of faith. In America, the worldview of Islam confronts American notions of space and its appropriations in interesting ways, especially within the African American Muslim home. In this section, we will examine how domestic space in African American Muslim communities is constituted differently as compared to homes in the general American population. My primary information will be drawn from Darul Islam and Islamic Party communities, and the reader should bear in mind that I am presenting a composite picture based on evidence gathered in these communities, rather than a structuring of home life that is strictly adhered to by all African American Muslims.

African American Muslim homes are at once spaces of culture formation and separation. Culture formation is exemplified in the synthesis of a variety of Muslim cultural norms with American cultural norms. Separation is achieved through the strict demarcation of domestic space from the space of Darul Harb ("the House of War"), a space that is rife with religious intolerance and racism. In attempting to facilitate these dual objectives of culture formation and separation, African American Muslims have continually attempted to replicate the earliest Muslim communities by locating themselves and their homes in close proximity to the masjid. When possible, small apartment buildings near the masjid are purchased. In some cases, entire communities have moved to rural areas to achieve the social cohesion and protection engendered by physical togetherness.

In general, there is only one technical requirement for Muslim space—i.e., a place for prayer. This place must have two dimensions

—the internal space, into which the Muslim retreats for experiencing *taqwa* for *salat*, and an external space, where the Muslim can face the Ka'aba and perform the prayer unmolested. As a primary consideration both spaces should be free from pollution. This basic requirement of a place for prayer is at the core of the arrangement of domestic space, an arrangement which, in the Muslim consciousness, represents power and knowledge in Islam.

For African American Muslims, lack of control over the architectural design of their homes and the typical absence of a physical enclave of Muslim houses makes identification of Muslim space a necessity. Thus, African American Muslim homes are typically first distinguished at their doorways, by either a sticker bearing an Islamic saying or by some Arabic calligraphy. This public announcement and permanent display of difference expresses an "other" (i.e., non-American) allegiance, and indicates the creation of a boundary where the locus of control is on the inside, not on the outside. We might say that the sign dictates an attitude. It says that, in this house, the hostile environment of racism, discrimination, and religious intolerance are locked out. To visitors, it signals both a welcome and a warning.

Without a definable seat in the Muslim world—that is, an already established cultural appropriation of Islam developed over centuries—many African American Muslims have had the entire Muslim world as a frame of reference for interior design. To the notion of space we can add the discussion of time. The tension created between time in the West and time in Islam also has its most prominent effects in domestic space. For example, activity in Muslim homes begins with the pre-dawn prayer while most non-Muslim neighbors are sleeping. A further example is fasting during the month of Ramadan, which necessitates a different order in the Muslim home—a predawn meal is eaten; the fast is broken at sunset (usually with other families) and night prayers are longer, performed either at home or in the *masjid*. To outsiders it must seem as if day and night have been reversed.

Temporality becomes an important aspect of living in that there is constant movement between realities. From exhortations to pray:

> Establish worship at the going down of the sun until the dark of night, and (the recital of) the Qur'an at dawn. Lo! (the recital of) the Quar'an at dawn is ever witnessed. (17:78)

to the fast:

> O ye who believe! Fasting is prescribed for you, even as it was prescribed for those before you, that ye may ward off (evil). (2:183)

along with the constant superimposition of a totally "other" understanding of time:

> One day He will gather them together: (It will be) as if they had tarried but an hour of a day... (10:45)

In "overlapping universes," Muslims have often negotiated both their personal and domestic space. At work, prayer time/space is often obtained at the sacrifice of lunch or breaktime. On the other hand, the carefully guarded domestic space is more than occasionally opened up to non-Muslims for a variety of everyday reasons. The universe of American life has its demands of both time and space which though overlapping with the time and space of Islam, frequently are in tension.

All of these factors have led to the emergence of a community that is clearly visible and at the same time invisible to its neighbors.

Except when visitors are present, the home is a private area that is gender-neutral space. Women are free in the space of their homes to unveil and wear clothing that is revealing and/or stylish, as may be prescribed by any adult males present. Windows are covered due to the close proximity of neighbors in most urban areas. Without this measure, neighbors could readily observe within the home what only the immediate family can see of the women according to Islamic injunctions. When visitors are present, traditional garb is worn and gender separations is observed.

Decades of immigrant influence has led to specific models of domestic space in African American Muslim communities. Cleanliness and minimal consumption are hallmarks, in accordance with the austerity practiced by the Prophet Muhammad in his own home. Entrance into Muslim space requires the removal of one's shoes; this etiquette is observed in all communities. Baskets, shoe racks, bookcases, crates, or just a designated space near the front door all serve to collect shoes. Other foot covering for wear inside the home is generally not provided. Women typically carry an extra pair of socks with them to put on when visiting. For visitors, entrance also marks off the beginnings of gendered space, because from the point of entry to a home women are escorted to one portion of the house, while men are escorted to another. The members of the household also divide themselves along gender lines at this point.

Once inside the house the visitor notices that the walls of the home are covered with Arabic calligraphy in various scripts, framed as well as unframed. Visitors might also observe bronze plates, engraved with various Qur'anic *suras* (the basic units of recitation), and synthetic Oriental carpets. The presence and type of furnishings vary, and depend on the interpretation of the aforementioned austerity practiced by the Prophet Muhammad. In some homes, the furnishings for seating may remind the visitor of the seating one readily finds in a Moroccan restaurant—fat pillows made from synthetic Oriental rugs, with tables no more than a foot tall. In other homes, tables have no legs, or mattresses may serve as places to sit. Still other homes have traditional American furnishings, arranged in an Oriental or Middle-Eastern manner. The period from 1980 to 1982 saw a change in the fabric used to cover pillows from Indian subcontinent mirrored fabrics and oriental designs to African fabrics (without images).[5] In many homes African wooden instruments have also taken the place of brass vases. In most living rooms, the latest copies of various Muslim newspapers, journals, and pamphlets are in view. Rarely are there issues of *Time*, *Ebony*, *Essence*, or *Woman's Day* magazines on hand. Windows shades, curtains, and drapes are always drawn closed.

Bookcases are a mainstay of living rooms. The *Qur'an* is always on the top shelf by itself. There is at least one set of *hadith* and several sets of commentary—Maulana Ali's and/or Yusuf Ali's—just below them. The remaining texts are usually of a confessional nature, generally written in Pakistan or Egypt. These books are generally purchased from merchants, the *masjid*, and conventions. Also typically, either on the bookcase or on a table, are *dhikr* beads. The prayer rugs and veils are also usually kept in the living room. In homes where the living room is the primary or only true public space, the bookcase is sometimes used to configure the room toward Mecca. If the bookcase is not used in this manner, the *qiblah* (direction toward the Ka'aba in Mecca) is indicated by some other piece of furnishing or by a wall plaque. Muslims in the house face that symbol as they pray.

There is usually a concerted effort in these homes to keep living room furniture to a minimum. This is in order to afford the easy rearrangement of the furnishings to convert the living-room space into prayer space. In contrast, dining rooms are usually fully furnished, provided that there is an extra room that can serve as prayer room. In the absence of an additional room, however, the dining room, along with the living room, becomes a prayer area.

When there are visitors the kitchen space is designated for the women, while the men eat and pray in the living room. If the number of men is large, the dining room space is used to accommodate the overflow from the living room. In either case, the women are relegated to the kitchen, with all of its attendant discomforts. It should be noted, however, that in the communities I examined there is a growing discomfort with this adaptation from the Muslim world, and change is occurring as individuals begin to acknowledge the necessity of women's participation in conversations on organization and politics, in addition to purely religious discussions.

In the communities that I observed, the most remarkable feat of culture-building was exemplified in the unique collection of decorator objects and Muslim understandings found within the home. An enthusiastic mixture of worlds is displayed in living rooms that contain Berber-patterned rugs accenting rattan furniture, and

Victorian lamps alongside Indian brass vases and Arabic calligraphy. Permutations of Arabic overlaid with black English have expanded the classical language in interesting ways—for example, the word *masha'allah*, which is generally understood to mean "it is what Allah decreed" and to denote happiness over some occurrence, is used by some African American Muslims negatively, as a lament. In their domestic spaces, African American Muslims have thus taken small portions of various Muslim cultures and woven an interesting tapestry that transcends (without denying) both their American nationality and their ethnicity. They have, in short, created a space for Islam inside the boundaries of Western architecture and culture.

CHILDREN

The majority of African American Muslim parents strive diligently to "build in our children Islamic personalities and Islamic attitudes through an Islamically oriented family life."[6] At the birth of the child all Muslim fathers recite the *shahada*, beginning the child's relationship with Allah, which the parents hope to nourish. The *akeeka* is the celebration of the birth of the child and the naming ceremony. At this time, parents usually slaughter a lamb, in order to feed the people present at the ceremony, and to distribute to families in the community as *sadaqa*.

The mother is able to begin praying again as soon as possible after childbirth, and the child is usually placed on the prayer rug with her, so that the space of prayer is transferred to him or her. As the Muslim child grows up he/she is expected to participate, at an appropriate level, in all the daily obligations. When children are too young to pray, they are expected to come to prayer and sit; most parents constantly recite portions of the *Qur'an*, so that children will mimic them. Children are taught early what they can and cannot eat; what kinds of behavior are unlawful; what they can and cannot wear; what kind of language is good to use; politeness to elders; and some Arabic phrases such as a greeting or thank-you.

At a time before puberty (in some communities at seven, in other communities between nine and eleven), the girls are separated from the boys in the public space. Puberty is the time when praying five times daily, fasting during Ramadan, reading the *Qur'an*, and understanding charity becomes obligations (though not quite at the same level as adults). Girls will begin to go to parties for girls only, and boys will be taken out for sports with men. Gender-specific information is transmitted during this time.

African American Muslims are seriously concerned with the education of their children. This concern is on at least two levels—religious and social. Almost all communities have a weekend school of some sort for the continuous Islamic education of their children. Several communities have schools that range from the kindergarten to the twelfth grade. There are to date at least four Islamic colleges—in Illinois, New York, South Carolina, and Virginia. In recent years, several educators from different communities have convened to standardize the texts and materials used from kindergarten to twelfth grade in Muslim schools.[7]

Muslim children who attend public schools in the United states often face a challenge. This challenge usually begins with teachers who refuse to pronounce their names and demand that they "get a nickname." Young Muslim girls are often subjected to ridicule if they wear scarves to school, and in some cases are asked to remove them. The most difficult situations for children arise when, beginning at the ages of eight or nine, public-school teachers understand that a part of education is preparing children for dating. Children are asked to simulate dates in the classroom, by preparing for an evening of dancing, dressing in evening or formal attire, and so on. Muslim children have been threatened and ridiculed because most Muslim parents take offense at this behavior and refuse to allow their children to participate. This usually results in poor grades for their children on these projects.

In some states, Muslims have filed lawsuits with regard to being forced to participate in such school events, as well as over the treatment in history texts of Muslims. African American Muslim parents have a dual complaint: African Americans are poorly represented in texts, and Muslims are represented in a distorted manner, when they are mentioned at all. Thus far, with the possible exception of California, few publishers of history texts have taken these complaints seriously; thus, this battle continues.

All Muslim parents are concerned with the violence and sex that appears daily on American television and in the schools. This has led some parents to take on the task of home schooling, while others who have put their children in public schools take them out at puberty. Unfortunately, this rarely solves the problems. As a result, many communities have turned their attention to organizing activities for youth and finding ways to include them in the daily activities of masajid. Most parents find themselves, like other American parents, overwhelmed by what passes for normal social mores of sex in adolescence, prevalent drug use among teens, and they worry about the possibilities of their children being victimized. In many communities, Muslim parents have joined with Christian and Jewish parents in organizing efforts to protect their children from the violence and drugs in neighborhoods.

In Islam, marriage is the only permissible way of fulfilling sexual urges. No extramarital sex is allowed, and all extramarital relationships are looked upon harshly—in some communities, such relationships are punished according to Islamic law, by lashings. While there is generally no community penalty, Muslim parents pay a great deal of attention to their children's level of sexuality. It is felt that American society is far too permissive with respect to the sexual relationships of children, and Muslim parents find little support in their drive to keep boys and girls separated until they at least near the age of marriage. Although there is little public talk of dating, sex, abortion, or contraception, there are plenty of private discussions.

Public schools, however, include sex education in their regular curricula, and the issue arises continually. Some parents have opted to marry off daughters early, at ages sixteen to eighteen in an attempt to prevent the temptation of a sexual relationship. Others have pushed higher education to their children as a goal before marriage, hoping that the rigors of studying will leave little energy for relationships.

CELEBRATIONS

Major celebrations are particular to each of the various African American Islamic communities are group particular. The Moorish Science Temple celebrates the Prophet's Birthday on January 8 of each year, and begin their New Year on January 15.

> The Prophet's birthday is a special occasion in all temples. Full Moorish regalia is worn by those members who can afford it, and there is likely to be feasting and distribution of gifts as in Christmas celebrations. A number of unconverted guests are invited.[9]

The Moorish Science community also makes note of the anniversaries of its two major organizations—the Young People's Moorish National League and the Moorish National Sisters Auxiliary, which were both founded in 1928.

The Nation of Islam's major celebration is Saviour's Day, which is a celebration of Fard Muhammad's birthday on February 26 of each year. This community had generally celebrated Ramadan (the month of fasting for Muslims around the world—the month when the first portions of the *Qur'an* were revealed to Prophet Muhammad ibn Abdullah) in December to discipline members against the glitz of Christmas. Recently, some members of this community have participated in Ramadan as the lunar month with the rest of the Muslim world, but have not joined in the celebrations at the end of Ramadan or the *hajj*.

Major celebrations among the rest of the Islamic communities are the Eid al-Fitr and Eid al-Adha. Eid al-Fitr occurs as a three day feast/festival at the end of the Fast of Ramadan. In America, this is the Eid Feast best planned for which regard to taking time off work or school for at least one day. On this occasion gifts are purchased for members of the family, for relatives, and *zakat* is paid in the community. The Eid al-Adha is celebrated at the end of the *hajj* which is about 10 weeks after the end of Ramadan. The accompanying festivities are more low-key but nevertheless it is a time for visiting and feasts.

FUNERALS

The final aspect of family life comes at death, in the form of established funeral practices. The body is immediately, or as soon as possible after death, prepared for the funeral prayer (*janaaza*). The funeral prayer then takes place, usually in the *masjid* or a funeral home. Finally, there is a funeral procession to the burial site, and the body is buried.

After the person is declared dead, the body is washed by the procedure of modified *wudu* and *ghusl.* Females wash the body of other females, and males wash males. The body is washed with soap and water. Perfumed oil is added to the water of the washing for scent. Embalming is not permitted. The body is then enshrouded—males with three pieces of muslin cloth, and females, with four pieces of cloth (the same material used on *hajj*). At the time of burial, the body is laid on its right side, with the head toward Mecca. At the grave site, after a few shovels or scoops of dirt have been thrown on top of the plain coffin or shrouded body, someone speaks, reminding the deceased of the truth of the *shahadah* (i.e., of the Oneness of Allah, and that Muhammad is His Messenger); the guidance provided by the *Qur'an*; and the duties of the *ummah* (community of believers).[9]

While in some Muslim countries there are customs of meals, Qur'anic recitations, and so on at various periods up to forty days after death and then at periodic times afterward, African American Muslims as a community mourn for an unspecified time and immediately focus on the care of the family of the deceased.

In America there is a need to have death certified. If the person dies in the streets, a public place, or the hospital, there is the normal procedure for pronouncement of death by certified medical personnel. If the person dies at home, the appropriate authorities are notified so that they can make a pronouncement of death, and then the Islamic rites are performed. There are instances where the relatives of the deceased are not Muslim and prefer another religious ceremony, and their will prevails if the deceased did not indicate that he/she wished to be buried as a Muslim or write a will to that effect. In some cities and rural areas, Muslims have cemeteries or have purchased tracts of space within privately owned burial grounds. Most recently, in African American Muslim communities there is a widespread effort to encourage families to join a *janaaza* plan. The Janaaza Planning Program, located in Chicago, is a not-for-profit corporation. This program endeavors to enable Muslims "to pre-plan and fund final arrangements before the time of need,"[10] and constitutes another instance where American ways and Islamic rites have been synthesized.

Social Issues and Challenges: The Tension between Darul Islam and Darul Harb

وَلَوْ شَاءَ اللَّهُ لَجَعَلَهُمْ أُمَّةً وَاحِدَةً وَلَٰكِن
يُدْخِلُ مَن يَشَاءُ فِي رَحْمَتِهِ وَالظَّالِمُونَ مَا لَهُم
مِّن وَلِيٍّ وَلَا نَصِيرٍ ٨

And if Allah had pleased He would surely have made them a single community, but He makes whom He pleases enter into His mercy, and the unjust it is that shall have no guardian or helper.

—Sura Shura 42:8.

As previous chapters have indicated, African American Muslims are constantly aware of their choice of Islam versus the choice of a more mainstream religion, and they must struggle to nourish spirituality on a daily basis in a largely hostile environment. While Islamic spirituality is enhanced by adhering to the five pillars, spending time and building solidarity with other Muslims, engaging in extensive Islamic study, a certain degree of interaction with non–Muslim America is unavoidable, and this interaction with the "Darul Harb" gives rise to a variety of challenges. This chapter will examine some of the major social challenges that confront African American Muslims as they interact with the educational, legal, and economic systems of mainstream America.

EDUCATIONAL CHALLENGES

A series of issues and concerns have arisen over the years with respect to the Muslim community and public education. Quality education and safety for children has been one of most prominent concerns. African American Muslims generally view the public school system in the United States as a space of selective learning which is hostile toward difference and often violent. Kamal Ali aptly summarizes the tension between Islam and mainstream American education as follows:

> The absence of prayer in school, the decidedly Western interpretation of history and the social studies, the highly competitive and materialistic school subculture, and the overall orientation of the public-school goals and activities around a protean Judeo-Christian standard are, in combination, a challenge and an effort to long established Islamic educational ideals.[1]

As one might expect, the absence of prayer and explicit moral instruction in public schools is especially troubling from an Islamic perspective. While American society relegates such practices to the home, Muslims believe that prayer and moral instruction must be reiterated in schools, in order to provide a sense of discipline, continuity, and cohesion in the lives of children. Although there is growing support in the general American population in favor of school prayer, such sentiment is of course aimed toward including Judeo-Christian rather than to Islamic prayer practices.

Western approaches to history and the social sciences are also regarded as highly problematic by Muslims. The Prophet Muhammad and Islamic civilization are seldom mentioned, and when they are it is usually in a denigrating context. In general, Muslim children in public schools across America are educated to believe that they have no place in the scope of world history, and that Islam has made no significant contributions to world histor., The vast majority of texts for junior and senior high school students use recent events to characterize the "backwardness" and barbarity of Muslims. Recently, there have been widespread concerted efforts by Muslims to change how publishers treat Islam in texts, and to alter and expand the information teachers have regarding Islam and Muslims. In particular, the Council on Islamic Education, founded and directed by Shabbir Mansuri, has focused on educating the major educational publishers regarding Islam. Many university professors of Islamic studies and/or Middle Eastern studies have also formulated programs to educate teachers from elementary to high schools on Islam and related topics.

The highly competitive and materialistic school subculture and its increasingly violent nature also presents a dilemma for Muslims who are trying to live according to Islamic ideals but are unable to afford private education. Although American schools typically permit flexibility with regard to student dress and fashion, ranging from skin-tight to baggy clothing, this flexibility often does not extend to Muslims, as an attitude of intolerance has pervaded in regard to "Islamic" dress, which usually takes the form of veils and long shirts.

The issue of health education turned sex education is likewise of serious concern for Muslim parents with children in public schools. Many school systems presume that all teenagers are or will be sexually active, and seek to educate young people about pregnancy, single parenthood, venereal diseases, and the use of contraception. Since most school districts until very recently did not give parents a say about this required course, this issue has led many parents to find ways to afford private education. Some Muslim parents have joined non-Muslim parents in protests over this concern, especially since sex education has become a part of the curriculum of elementary schools.

One other area of concern for Muslims revolves around curricula dealing with both Judeo-Christian and secular holidays. Even though prayer has been banned from schools, religious activities have not been completely curtailed. Students are educated into the stories of Christmas, Passover, Easter, and Halloween. These activities are not extracurricular, and the requirement of student participation is a burden on Muslim students, whose celebrations are not even mentioned. Increasing movement toward multicultural education has not yet had an effect on this portion of the curriculum in public schools.

EDUCATIONAL ALTERNATIVES

> Islamic school theory rests on concepts that allow for individual achievement within defined cultural limits. The assumption is that the sum of all possible acquired skills, knowledge and resources are valuable only to the degree they enhance the communities' ability to serve God.[2]

Muslims have sought several alternatives to either replace or supplement the public-school experience. "Sunday" schools, Qur'anic schools, correspondence courses, full-time day schools, boarding schools, and college preparatory schools are among the current list of Muslim endeavors. Several areas of problems have emerged in connection with these educational alternatives, but the most prevalent has been the issue of texts, both Islamic and secular. For African American children the few series of Islamic texts and workbooks available in English have little if any reference to them and their communities. African American Muslim educators have begun to look closely at this emerging problem as a subset of the larger problems of the serious shortage of English texts on Islamic subjects for children. What the Islamic curriculum should contain is another area of concern.

Most communities have some sort of weekend school on Saturday and/or Sunday with a core of instruction for both children and adults. The curriculum in such schools consists of Arabic language, memorization and recitation of the *Qur'an*, instruction in *wudu* (ablution) and *salat* (formal prayer), Islamic history, and *sirah* literature (biographies of the Prophet Muhammad). Full-time schools in Muslim communities have to meet the criteria of state certification with regard to facilities, teachers, and curriculum. In such full-time Islamic schools, there is a serious lack of texts which uphold values that Muslims find totally acceptable. Teachers must therefore spend a great deal of time adding the concepts of God and morality to the curriculum and addressing the negative stereotypes of Muslims in the social sciences. It is only very recently that American Muslim educators have come together to create a national school board. As the quality of public-school instruction decreases and the violence in the public school system continues to increase, the number of Muslim schools has steadily increased.

The demand for African American Muslim schools is very much on the rise but, unfortunately, supply does not yet meet demand. The closing of the Sister Clara Muhammad Schools has left a vacuum that has not been filled. In response to this situation, an ever-increasing number of parents are devoting their resources to home-schooling programs registered with the state. African American Muslims are largely on their own in this important educational endeavor, as immigrant communities have generally chosen not to associate themselves with African American Muslim schools, and have channeled most of their resources into building schools of their own.

LEGAL CHALLENGES: THE PENAL SYSTEM

A growing concern for African American Muslim communities centers around United States law and its implications. The guiding force of Islam is a set of laws and authority that transcends the United States legal system. Oftentimes there is tension between the two. In Islam there is an "acknowledgment of God's authority over the conduct of man."

> Unlike its Western counterpart, Islamic jurisprudence is not confined to commands and prohibitions, and far less to commands which originate in a court of law. Its scope is much wider, as it is concerned no only with what a man must do or must not do, but also with what he ought not to do, and the much larger area where his decision to do or to avoid doing something is his own prerogative.[3]

In Islam, sovereignty rests with God. What is good, evil, right or wrong is determined by God. Values and "the laws which uphold those values" are determined by God.

> The Muslim community is entrusted with the authority to implement the Shari'ah, to administer justice and to take all necessary measures in the interest of good government. The sovereignty of the people, if the use of the word "sovereignty" is at all appropriate, is a delighted, or executive sovereignty (*Sultan Tanfidhi*) only. The role of the ballot box and the sovereignty of the people are thus seen in a different light in Islamic law to that of Western jurisprudence.[4]

Islam is a worldview in which the pervasiveness of religious law is felt continuously. Even though individual Muslims make choices about what to do or not do, it is always with a general awareness of Qur'anic injunctions. In contrast, United States Constitutional Law does not recognize religious law as primary, or even provides for the restriction of religious expression under certain circumstances.

> Although right to hold religious beliefs as guaranteed by the free exercise clause of the First Amendment is absolute, right to express beliefs is not and government may regulate the time, place and manner of privileged expression when regulation is reasonable and content-neutral and such expression may be otherwise restricted by government only when government can show that restrictive regulation or practice serves compelling governmental interest and is least restrictive means by which that interest effectively can be served.[5]

The greatest body of literature concerning the legal challenges that confront African American Muslims has emerged in the area of penology and related topics. The First Amendment has permitted incarcerated African American Muslims to establish case law. In a number of cases, Muslims have used the First Amendment to have their Muslim names acknowledged, to have a pork-free diet, and to wear kufis on their heads.[6] Since, technically, there are at least fifty different legal systems in the United states as well as a federal judicial system, a decision rendered by a judge in one state is not necessarily binding on any other, even on one in the same federal district. Thus, while rulings regarding names, pork-free diets and the right to wear clothing with religious significance are generally upheld, there are prisons where Muslim inmates will still have to go to court, arguing on the basis of case precedent. In many instances communities have assisted in these cases by providing financial or legal assistance.

Understanding Islam and its various expressions in the United States has been a challenge for prison administrators and staff. Since the majority religion is Christianity, with the rehabilitative understanding that inmates connect to religious (Christian) values

> Most prisons allow possession of the Bible, visits by and written communications with ministers of particular faiths, the receipt of religious materials, the holding of religious services, and the wearing of religious medals and medallions, Indeed, traditional Christian worship is encouraged in the belief that it reinforces conservative teachings with regard to sin, repentance, and redemption.[7]

In contrast, the practice of Islam has been viewed as problematic by prison officials, and Muslims have had to fight for the same rights accorded to members of the mainstream religious tradition. The struggle of Muslims in this area has had a broad impact on religious practice in American prisons.

> In the First Amendment area, Muslims were also instrumental in establishing new rights for prisoners of all religions. Any discussion of the right to worship in prison inevitably revolves around Muslims because both the content and practice of their religion were once perceived as a threat to the administration of the penal institution.[8]
>
> In their struggle for freedom of reli gion, Muslims initiated suits against the American penal system that encompassed three basic issues: The first was whether the various substantive rights requested, such as the right to possession of the Koran and the right to religious services in prison, are guaranteed by the First Amendment.

> The second was whether a prison discriminates against a particular variety of religious beliefs by permitting prisoners of some religions certain rights denied to Muslims. Finally, and of critical importance, the courts were called upon to rule on prison officials' claims that the various aspects of the practice establish a danger of substantial interference with the orderly functioning and discipline of the institution.[9]

Muslims have led challenges in a number of other areas, including the rights to religious services, religious counseling, religious literature, and special feeding hours during Ramadan. As of 1993, according to an unpublished study of African American Muslims in the state and federal prison systems, there are seven full-time Imams in the federal system of fifty-four institutions, and of the federal chaplains there are only two Muslims who hold supervisory positions for an estimated population of over four thousand federal Muslim inmates.[10] The standard program instituted for Muslim inmates by these Imans include: the five-times-daily prayers, *Jum'ah* prayer, *ta'leem* (educational classes), thirty-day fasting of Ramadan, and Arabic instruction. Problems remain concerning the lack of eligible and qualified Muslim chaplains, certification procedures for these Imams, and lack of community support for inmates—e.g., provision of ongoing rehabilitation and/or halfway-house programs.

To test some of the widely held beliefs about Muslims in prison I applied for and obtained permission to visit the United States Penitentiary at Marion—the highest-security prison in America. In this prison, there are forty-five prisoners who claim Islam as their religion in the federal records. I was able to get twenty-seven of these inmates to agree to be interviewed. In two days I was actually able to interview eighteen of them. These inmates stated that it was a myth the "conversion" to Islam was made because affiliation with

Islam afforded them some security. They asserted that although this belief was probably true some decades ago with the Nation of Islam, for contemporary prisoners the first affiliation is based on locating other inmates from the same hometown ("homies"). Amongst other things, these interviews showed that not all inmates were from low-income one-parent families; some even had legal professionals in their immediate families, along with school teachers and other white-collar professionals. I found that there was a good deal of diversity of community affiliation amongst the inmates—there were Moorish Science Temple Muslims, Nation of Islam Muslims, and "just" Sunni or Shiite Muslims. Inmates used different resources for their Islamic education. For example, Minister Farrakhan has produced a series of lectures for members of the Nation of Islam to study. At Marion, Muslim prisoners study assiduously, perhaps because of the lockdown situation that prevails twenty-three hours each day.

ADDITIONAL LEGAL ISSUES

Another prominent legal issue confronting African American Muslims has to do with the incorporation of Islamic law into their own unique historical and cultural context. Along these lines, there is widespread sentiment amongst African Americans that there needs to be a distinction between "things Islamic" and "things cultural," so that African American Muslims are not forced to inherit cultural influences from the rest of the Islamic world as they strive to incorporate Islamic law into their lives and communities. In attempting to resolve this issue, some African Americans have taken steps toward developing an American *madhab* (school of Islamic law).

Other areas of legal concern are centered on family law and inheritance rights. While several communities regard polygyny as a valid form of marriage, United States law of course holds a contrary view of the matter. From a legal standpoint, divorce and fair adjudication of marital wealth, child-custody decisions, and so on, remain under the jurisdiction of the American court system, which creates a problem for African American Muslims, who tend to dislike and distrust this system, and who often eschew it even when it could work to their advantage—for example, Muslim women in the midst of divorce proceedings often do not use the court system to ensure fair distribution of assets, alimony payments, child custody, and so on. Similar problems are faced in regard to inheritance. When a relative dies Muslim benefactors often find themselves faced with contradictions between United States and Islamic Law. If the relative is non-Muslim, concerns may also be raised about inheriting money or property that was earned in a.disreputable way—for example, through gambling or the sale of products that are forbidden to Muslims. Although there is a National Fiqh (jurisprudence) Council designed to deal with legal issues, the council is overwhelmingly composed of naturalized Muslims who have not found these problems important, and the problems have thus far gone unresolved.

THE MEDIA AND ISLAM

The media in African American Muslim communities consists of newspapers (the *Muslim Journal*, the *Final Call*, *Muhammad Speaks*), newsletters (*Al-Nisa*, *Shahabiyat*), cable television, and radio programs. These organs are filled with the concerns of the communities about issues in America and abroad. One standard category is the focus of Islamic instruction on the *Qur'an* and its commentary, Islamic history, and general interpretation of both for the community. All of the media seek information from the Muslim world, especially events and concerns not covered in the Western media. Most print mediums publish calendars of events around the country along with general paid advertisements. Editorial columns are used to raise issues and concerns both within and outside of the African American community.

Representations of Islam and Muslims in the mainstream media are of great concern to African American Muslims. Muslims have learned that the West not only depicts Islam as threatening and evil, but that its coverage of events involving Muslims has frequently fostered violent retaliatory acts against Muslims. Even though Muslims are divided over how much participation they want to have in the infrastructure of the United States, they all know that their lives are in danger once Americans become convinced that Muslims are terrorists. Interaction with the mainstream media is thus required to challenge and dispel such images.

African American Muslim communities have endured government spies, informants, attacks by the police, surveillance, and the attacks of anti-Islamic U.S. media since the early days of Noble Drew Ali and Elijah Muhammad, up to the assaults on individual African American Muslims after the bombing of the World Trade Center in 1992. Thus far, these efforts have cause significant damage, but have failed either to destroy or even prevent growth in Muslim communities. Communities involved in nation-building —e.g., the Nation of Islam—have received the bulk of the animosity produced in every corner of the media, while those whose focus includes *ummah* have received the general wrath reserved for Muslims of any ethnicity. Either way, African American Muslims have had a problematic existence in the West.

Recent media discourse has found headlines such as "Terrorism Comes to America," and talk-show hosts entertaining questions such as "Should We Americans Permit Muslims into the Country?" This trend seems to have begun during the days of the Iranian revolution and the hostage crisis, and has become increasingly strident. The height of this anti-Islamic fervor is seen most clearly in the image of then Vice President of the United States Dan Quayle asserting to a large audience before whom he was speaking that Islamic fundamentalism has replaced communism as the greatest threat to Western Democracy. In the 1990s, the media began what has become a systematized attack on Islam and Muslims, introducing the terms "fundamentalism," "terrorism," and "holy war" as being synonymous with Islam. Once these terms were coined, they were accepted by the media and the public as the only way to describe Muslims and their "fanatical" religion.

Subsequently, evidence has been sought to legitimate the depiction.

Salman Rushdie and his novel *The Satanic Verses* were used as a tool to prove that Islam had no ethics, and that Muslims were such "fundamentalists" that they were willing to kill over the publication of a text they had not even read. Islam was portrayed as the only religion which dared to have an ethical code that differed from the universal norm (the ethics, even if not upheld, of the West). Muslims across America were asked whether or not Salman Rushdie should be killed, as if their existence as human beings depended on an affirmation of the viewpoint of the West. For African American Muslims—the descendants of slaves who were killed for even attempting to write the alphabet—the questions about Rushdie were absurd. Most African American Muslims had not read the text, while those who had may not have had time to reflect on the implications of certain passages before the media descended upon them.

Writings on the oppression of Muslim women have become favored topics of feature stories around the nation. These writings have become classic researches, defining Muslim women in the West. The most famous feature story was done in the *Atlanta Constitution-Journal* in June 1992 by two female reporters. In this story ignorance about Islam and assumption of the superiority of Western gender relations seriously distorted the important issues that needed to be raised. The implications of Islam for women in the West were so profound that women bombarded the Muslim media with articles of protest, the Atlanta Council of Imams met with representatives of the newspaper, and there was a well-publicized debate between the authors and several Muslim women. These responses have not, however, prevented non-Muslim female journalists from pursuing career advancement by telling the stories of oppressed Muslim women.

The Gulf War and the unrelenting determination of George Bush to kill Saddam Hussein, even if it meant killing everyone in Iraq, sent a chilling message to American Muslim communities—and probably most Americans. Never before had an entire war been televised nor had genocide previously been made public as it was being (and continues to be) carried out. Even though the original conflict was pushed to the background and the validity of the competing claims never discussed, Muslims saw the hatred of the West for Islam and Muslims. They also saw the extent of American hegemony in Muslim territory.

The major media has not generally considered the events of the Muslim communities worthy reporting, with the exception of Louis Farrakhan's Nation of Islam. Even though this community comprises approximately one percent of the African American Muslim population, it has been elevated to a position of prominence by some in the American Jewish community and the media as representational of both Islam and African American Islam. In contrast, within the African American Muslim community as a whole, very little attention is paid to the Nation of Islam, and when any attention is given, the community is considered to be marginalized at best. Most African American Muslims, at least those interviewed for this text, agree with Farrakhan's primary goal of "black self-help" and his analysis of the economic and political status of African American, but deplore his refusal to move into a more normative Islamic stance with regard to the foundations of faith.

The current controversy with the American Jewish community has not reached its end and the hostilities are rising as of this writing. The Jewish community at his point has not chosen to dialogue with the larger community of African American Muslims, and has instead engaged the Black Christian community in order talk about its perceptions of Jews. Some leaders in African American Muslim communities are actively seeking dialogue to bring clarity to the situation, and we will have to see how their efforts work out.

ECONOMIC CHALLENGES

From an Islamic perspective, everything that exists in the universe is, in principle, the property of Allah Himself. There is, however, a series of things that He has given "equally to all men as common trust"—e.g., fire, water, earth, air, light, the animals for hunting, mines and unowned or uncultivated lands. These things are not the property of any individual, but part of a common trust and responsibility. Every human is the beneficiary of this trust and is entitled to its use. The moral and just use of nature is the responsibility of humankind. Accordingly, the economic activities that result from this use are an aspect of the fulfillment of mankind's responsibility.

In Islam, wealth is good and the pursuit of wealth is a legitimate aim of human behavior. As with other human activities, wealth, seen generally as a measure of success, is always associated with religion and moral values—it is a bounty from God that must be handled responsibly. Goods are conceived of as the useful, beneficial, consumable materials whose utilization brings about a combination of a moral, material, and spiritual enhancement. Items or concepts that do not fulfill these criteria at some level are not regarded as good, and are not considered either property or assets by Muslims. In Islam, economic utility requires that in addition to its "extrinsic quality," a thing must possess moral usefulness. Some products, (be they physical things or concepts) must be exchangeable and enhance the quality of life.

In Islam, individuals are understood to be the owners of the fruits of their labor and free agents with regard to transactions. There is neither unlimited freedom of private ownership, nor public ownership to an extent that negates individual interests. Rather, there is private ownership based on the freedom of private individuals, and public or collective ownership based on common resources and interests. In this ideal system, there is plenty of room for intelligent, hard-working individuals to compete in an open market, while at the same time the accumulation of wealth in one pair of hands is prevented. A sense of moral responsibility places restraints on the individual from within, while the law enacts restraints on the individual from without, thus resulting in each individual receiving his/her just share in the circulation of wealth. Wealth, then, is only a means to an end, not the end itself. The end is to worship God.

One control on wealth designed to encourage the distribution of it to the community is *zakat.*

> *Al-Zakat* is a special tax levied on the total net worth of an individual's property, to be collected by the state and spent for specific purposes, primarily the several types of social insurance.
>
> *Zakat* controls (a) the allocation of productive wealth among alternative uses, (b) the non-productive means of production, (c) the allocation of income between expenditure and saving, (d) the allocation of savings between productive uses and durable luxury goods, and (e) the long-run redistribution of wealth.[11]

Islamic economic principles raise many questions in connection with the economy of the West. An especially prominent ongoing issue is that of *riba* (usury). In Islam, usury is defined as an excess or addition over and above the principal sum lent. This definition "includes all kinds of interest, whether the rate be high or low, and whether the interest is or is not added to the principal sum, after fixed periods." In the Western banking/credit system, interest is an integral and primary part of the system. In the West, Muslims thus find themselves in a series of systems which are constructed to induce "the amassing of wealth instead of its distribution,"[12] and which run contrary to Islamic teaching concerning *riba.*

The nature and function of banks has prompted numerous discussions on usury and the moral character of the institution itself. People deposit money in banks because it is safe and because the bank acts as a monitor and account—within the regulations of the bank, the individual has access to and can withdraw his/her money on demand. But problems arise with regard to what is done with the money while it is in the bank. Of course banks do not simply store money—they draw profit from it, which in turn is invested, lent to others, paid out to depositors and shareholders. These activities are possible because of interest. The profit is not all invested, lent, or returned, because some is put into a fund to keep money in reserve and to insure against loss. From an Islamic perspective, the fact that the profit is not the result of work is problematic. That some banks invest in goods (material or conceptual) that are not morally useful is also dubious. One suggestion made by some scholars is that Muslims who use banks may give the excess amount received as interest on the deposits to charity. Another alternative is to form cooperative lending institutions where shareholders are depositors as well as borrowers.

POLITICAL CHALLENGES

In an article entitled "Political Activity of Muslims in America," Steve Johnson asserts that

> despite the growing number of Muslim immigrants attaining U.S. citizenship, and the fact that nearly 30 percent of all Muslims in the United States are indigenous American citizens, as a group Muslims remain essentially a political nonentity.[13]

For the most part, this statement remains true. African American Muslims remain divided, as do most African Americans, over whether or not there is any recourse to justice or representation in America for African Americans. Jesse Jackson's bid for the Democratic nomination for president in 1984 signaled the possibility for important changes in the American political scene, but at the same time its implications were ambivalent with regard to the political situation of African American Muslims. Few African American Muslim communities, if any, organized en masse to support Jackson's campaign, but individuals in record numbers registered to vote and were active in his campaign offices. Louis Farrakhan's Fruit of Islam provided protection for Jackson after he received a number of death threats, but Jackson's alliance with the

Nation of Islam apparently was political death for his campaign. Speculation abounded as to exactly what happened and why. Regardless of who did what, the message was clear on several levels —no association with Islam or any of its African American expressions is to be tolerated in a political campaign involving African Americans, at least not if the campaign endeavors to be successful.

Some African American Muslim communities desire to keep themselves separate from the American political arena. These communities advocate stabilizing the Muslim community as a priority. Examples of these communities include participants in the Darul Islam Movement. Nevertheless, while general Muslim disdain for American society has in the past prevented any active involvement, the present trend is leading toward persuasion by use of the vote. City and state politicians have seen the advantages in courting a block of Muslim votes, and are beginning to included the local masjid on their campaign routes.

With regard to the Muslim world, the awareness of politics has increased considerably amongst African American Muslims in the last few years. As the United States participates in or leads wars against Muslims, African American Muslims are paying more attention, and are getting involved in relief funds and other Muslim political agendas. African American Muslims are participating in crusades for Bosnia, Iraq, Sudan, Somalia, Pakistan, and Algeria with great energy. On the domestic front, however, African Americans do not hold positions of power in any of the major Muslim organizations, and thus will probably not be in a position to influence the political arena anytime in the near future unless communities ban together as voting blocks.

Women in Islam

وَمِنْ آيَاتِهِ أَنْ خَلَقَ لَكُم مِّنْ أَنفُسِكُمْ أَزْوَاجًا
لِّتَسْكُنُوا إِلَيْهَا وَجَعَلَ بَيْنَكُم مَّوَدَّةً وَرَحْمَةً
إِنَّ فِي ذَٰلِكَ لَآيَاتٍ لِّقَوْمٍ يَتَفَكَّرُونَ ﴿٢١﴾

And one of His signs is that He created mates for you from yourselves that you may find rest in them, and He put between you love and compassion; most surely there are signs in this for a people who reflect.

—Sura Rum 30:21.

DISCOURSES ON THE STATUS OF MUSLIM WOMEN

Muslim women and their roles in communities continue to be a major concern of both scholarly and everyday inquiry. To non-Muslims, Muslim women have been the subject of speculation, consternation, and ridicule for decades. As one Muslim teacher and scholar has noted:

> Old ideas about the place of women in Islam have hardly changed. The most difficult task I have faced in years of teaching Islam is how to provide an accurate account of the role of women in face of the deep prejudices of not only my students but also my colleagues. . . . And given the

> background of the students, it was natural for them to come into class convinced, on some level of their awareness, that Eastern women, and especially Muslim women, are the most oppressed and downtrodden women on earth, and that although Islam may have something interesting to say on some level, it certainly has nothing to offer on the level of women's role in society.[1]

Scholarly works have called Muslim women's existence and ways of being in the world as oppressed and voiceless, and have explored these characteristics in a variety of communities, elaborating a discourse replete with negative stereotypes. Western women feel that their "work on" Muslim women is a model of excellence.

> Our knowledge of women in Islamic society has benefited from the burgeoning studies on women in the West. This interest has resulted in excellent monographs, essay collections, scholarly and popular articles, and translations of works by Muslim women into Western languages, particularly English.[2]

Muslim women, however, are generally unflattered by such scholarship. For example, Leila Ahmed had complained that

> The peculiar practices of Islam with respect to women had always formed part of the Western narrative of the quintessential otherness and inferiority of Islam.[3]

> Broadly speaking, the thesis of the discourse on Islam blending a colonialism committed to male dominance with feminism—the thesis of the new colonial discourse of Islam centered on women—was that Islam was innately and immutably oppressive to women, that the veil and segregation epitomized that oppression, and that these customs were the fundamental reasons for the general and comprehensive backwardness of Islamic societies. [4]

This is not to imply that Muslim women in many Muslim cultures are not struggling to break bonds that prevent them from intellectual pursuits and physical mobility. Yet whereas many social scientists asserted a need to liberate Muslim women from their families, husbands, children, history, and culture, liberation for Muslim women is mostly conceived of in terms of the veil, often called *hijab*, and their role in the home. Muslim women scholars, fighting patriarchy have devoted considerable energy to clarifying the emergence of *hijab* as defining for Muslim women. Fatima Mernissi has explored this issue at length.

> The *hijab*—literally "curtain"—"descended," not to put a barrier between a man and a women . . . The descent of the hijab is an event dating back to verse 53 of Surah 33, which was revealed during year 5 of the Hejira (627 A.D.).
>
> "O you who believe! Enter not the Prophet's house for a meal without waiting for the proper time, unless

> permission be granted you. But when you are invited, enter; and when your meal is ended, then disperse. Linger not for conversation. Lo, that would cause annoyance to the Prophet, and he would be shy of (asking) you (to go); but Allah is not shy of the truth. And when you ask of them (the wives of the Prophet) anything, ask it of them from behind a curtain. That is purer for your hearts and for their hearts."[5]

Mernissi further illustrates another major use of the word *hijab* in *Qur'an* in *Sura* 41 *ayah* 5:

> And they say, "Our hearts are (fortified) within a covering against that (Book) towards which you call us. We are deaf in the ear and there exists a barrier between us and you. So carry on your work (according to your creed) and surely you are the workers (in accordance with our own doctrines)."[6]

In light of these Qur'anic passages, Mernissi concludes:

> So it is strange indeed to observe the modern course of this concept. . . . The very sign of the person who is damned, excluded from the privileges and spiritual grace to which the Muslim has access, is claimed in our day as a symbol of Muslim identity, manna for the Muslim woman.[7]

Muslim women scholars are not alone in seeking to clarify the identity of women although the emphases and roles outlined are sometimes different. Afzular Rahman asserts that

> It seems quite fair and rational to say that the circle of operation of woman in general is the home, while the field of work of man is outside the home. In other words, the basic and fundamental function of woman is to run the home. She is equipped with such natural gifts and capabilities as are suitable for the bringing up, nursing, education and training of children.[8]
>
> But woman is not called upon that scale and with that urgency to undertake social and collective obligations which would entail her leaving her household duties . . . it is more important for a woman to continue doing her household duties than to participate in collective worship.[9]

Dr. Hasan Al-Turabi, a Sudanese scholar and statesman, has contributed significantly to the issue of women and gender relations in a pamphlet entitled, *Women in Muslim Society and Islam.* Some of Dr. Al-Turabi's key observations are cited below.

> Men purposefully attempt to keep women weak, and the jealousy which they entertain in respect to women induces them to multiply the means for restraining and monopolizing them. They dominate the property and life of women out of vanity and arrogance.
>
> The greatest injustice visited upon

women is their segregation and isolation from the general society. Sometimes the slightest aspect of her public appearance is considered a form of obscene exhibitionism. Even her voice is bracketed in the same category. Her mere presence at a place where men are also present is considered shameful promiscuity. She is confined to her home in a manner prescribed in Islam only as a penal sanction for an act of adultery. She is so isolated on the pretext that she should devote herself exclusively to the care of her children and the service of her husband. But how can she qualify for attending to domestic family affairs or for the rearing of children in satisfactory manner without being herself versed through education or experience, in the moral and functional culture of the wider society?

So far as the familiar Hijab is concerned, it refers to the special regulations pertaining to the Prophet's wives due to their status and situation. They occupied a position different from all other women, and their responsibilty was therefore stiffened. God ordained that their reward, as well as their punishment would be double that for any other woman.

The verses of the same Sura ordained that the wives of the Prophet draw a curtain (to ensure privacy in the

> prophet's room which naturally attracted many visitors of all sorts), and that they dress up completely without showing any part their bodies including face and hands to any man; though all other Muslim women were exempted from these restrictions.[10]

Along similar lines, Rashid al-Ghanushi finds that in a close review of different *tafseers* (commentaries on the *Qur'an* and *hadith*), the view of women that is elaborated is incompatible with predominant cultural views.[11]

In attempting to sort out the controversial literature on the status of Muslim women, the most obvious questions to raise include: What actually does the *Qur'an* say about women? If there is a difference between the Qur'anic discourse and the cultural practices of Muslims, why is this so, given the fact that Muslims understand the *Qur'an* to be the word of God? If Muslims believe the *Qur'an* to be the authority for the social life, how could they misinterpret it so seriously?

In order to answer these important questions, Muslim women scholars are beginning to meticulously investigate what the *Qur'an* says and what has happened. In a text entitled, *Qur'an and Woman,* Amina Wadud-Mushin has made the following observations:

> Compatible mutually supportive functional relationships between men and women can be seen as part of the goal of the Qur'an with regard to society. However, the Qur'an does not propose or support a singular role or single definition of a set of roles, exclusively, for each gender across every culture.[12]

> Man and woman are two categories of the human species given the same or

> equal consideration and endowed with the same or equal potential. . . . The Qur'an encourages all believers, male and female, to follow their belief with actions, and for this it promises them a great reward.[13]
>
> The roles of women who have been referred to in the Qur'an fall into one of three categories: (1) A role which represents the social, cultural, and historical context in which that individual lived—without compliment or critique from the text. (2) A role which fulfills a universally accepted (i.e., nurturing or caretaking) female function, to which exceptions can be made—and have been made even in the Qur'an itself. Finally, (3) A role which fulfills a non-gender-specific function.[14]

Why is the contemporary discourse on women (there are no texts on men) so full of conflicting claims? Leila Ahmed has observed that "discourses shape and are shaped by specific moments in specific societies," which means that we have to look to Islamic history for an answer to this question.

> Converts brought traditions of thought and custom with them. For instance (to give just one example of how easily and invisibly scriptural assimilation could occur), in its account of the creation of humankind the Qur'an gives no indication of the order in which the first couple was created from Adam's rib. In Islamic traditionalist literature, however, which was inscribed in the period

> following the Muslim conquests, Eve, sure enough, is referred to as created from a rib.[15]
>
> The adoption of the veil by Muslim women occurred by similar process of seamless assimilation of the mores of the conquered people. . . . During Muhammed's (pbuh) lifetime and only toward the end at that, his wives were the only Muslim women required to veil. After his death and following the Muslim conquest of the adjoining territories, where upper-class women veiled, the veil became a commonplace item of clothing among Muslim upper-class women, by a process of assimilation that no one has yet ascertained in much detail.[16]

Dr. Al-Turabi has offered similar observations along these lines:

> Throughout history, Muslims have experienced a significant deviation from the general ideals of life as taught by Islam. . . . Whenever weakness creeps into the faith of Muslim men, they tend to treat women oppressively and seek to exploit them. This is a natural tendency, and is amply demonstrated by the fact that most of the rulings of the Qur'an regarding women were set down as restrictions on men—to prevent them from transgressing against women, as is their natural disposition and their actual practice in most societies.

> This discriminatory attitude of interpretation is very widespread. Yet another aspect of this tendentious jurisprudence is to generalize the provisions of the Qur'an and the Sunna that were meant to apply exclusively to the Prophet or his wives due to their unique position.[17]

While we do not have all the pieces to this puzzle, some Muslim scholars are examining Islamic history, philosophy, and commentaries on the *Qur'an* and *hadith* to find answers. Interpretations of the Qur'anic message, like all interpretations, are an exercise in power and knowledge. In the early days of Islam, debate and controversy filled the air, and from this atmosphere schools of thought formed. Eventually, we were left with five schools of legal thought, a few well-known philosophers, and one interpretation of the *Qur'an*. As Dr. Al-Turbi writes:

> Although the message of Islam spread in [Arab, Persian, and Indian] societies from early times, the teaching and inculcation of Islamic cultural values was not coextensive with the horizontal expansion. Consequently, some pre-Islamic values and prejudices, have contiued to persist despite the domination of Islamic forms.
>
> By attaching an Islamic value to these practices, they sought to give them legitamacy and sanctity, because the values of Islam were accepted as sacred and supreme. This explains the unabated influence, on the minds of many otherwise good Muslims, of attitudes abhorent to Islam.[18]

In the end, Muslim women were encased in a mold called "Muslim woman" which was ahistorical, silent, and without a strong Qur'anic basis.

ISLAM IN THE LIVES OF AFRICAN AMERICAN WOMEN

Before we examine how African-American women walk into this fourteen-hundred-year-old history, we need to know a few things about them. We must first address the issue of silence, on which bell hooks has aptly commented in her work *Talking Back*.

> This empasis on woman's silence may be an accurate remembering of what has taken place in the households of women from WASP backgrounds in the United States, but in black communities . . . women have not been silent. Their voices can be heard. Certainly for black women, our struggle has not been to emerge from silence into speech but to change the nature of our speech, to make a speech that compels listeners, one that is heard.[19]

African-American women as a whole have not seen themselves as silenced by their circumstances, though many times they have been hostage to the need to survive. They have always carefully chosen what they share, because the "sharing is always an issue of survival." African-American women have had to constantly fight the issues of racism, and even though they are aware of sexism, racism has been the commanding force. As hooks points out,

> Many black women insist that they do not join the feminist movement

> because they cannot bond with white women who are racist. . . .
>
> At times, the insistence that feminism is really "a white female thing that has nothing to do with black women" masks black female rage towards white women, a rage rooted in the historical servant-served relationship where white women have used power to dominate, exploit, and oppress. Many black women share this animosity, and it is evoked again and again when white women attempt to assert control over us.[20]

African-American women have, in large numbers, spurned the women's liberation movement and the feminist movement even though they have gained a little from both. African-American women have been formed socially by racism. Their spiritually has rarely been examined except through narratives of heroic deeds—usually either for family or the race.

The first Islamic encounter for African-American women was predominately in communities, where 'asabiya was the focus. During the first half of the twentieth century, for most African-American Muslim women, who generally had not encountered their Muslim sisters from the Muslim world, there is an ambiguous gender relationship. Women have a lot of say in nation-building—they are present, sometimes in quasi-leadership capacities, keeping the mini-nations informed and intact. At the same time, however, they are subject to the attitudes about women held by the men. For example, even though Clara Muhammad tended the Nation of Islam in its early days when Elijah Muhammad was jailed or running from the police, she is rarely written about, and leads no organizations within the Nation. For women in the Moorish Science Temple and the First Mosque of Pittsburgh, subordination of women is not so clearly a problem, but we have no written accounts of the first women and their lives. Women wear a modest dress and cover their heads, but do not seem to feel oppressed; rather, their dress is viewed as a difference that aligns them with a worldview, an identity other than slavery, and God.

The second half of the twentieth century brings a wave of Muslim immigrants into contact with already established African-American Islamic expressions. Along with these Muslim immigrants comes the notion of "Muslim woman," which includes silence, submissiveness, and absence. For some African-American Muslim women and for some of those moving into Islam, this notion is enticing, while for others it is the beginning of a new struggle.

The notion "Muslim woman" refers directly to dress and adab. The Muslim woman is one who looks Muslim, wearing a scarf that covers her hair, neck, and bosom. Her dress touches the ground, her sleeves close at the wrist, and whether she wears a blouse and pants or a dress her clothing must be loose enough so that it does not show her form. The Muslim woman is obedient to her husband, takes constant care of her children, and soft spoken. She does not want much, is content, and understands that this behavior is pleasing to God. Her obligations as a Muslim are marginalized. If she does not look like a Muslim woman she is not a Muslim woman, even if she prays five times daily, pays *zakat*, fasts during Ramadan, and saves to make *hajj*. This conception of Muslim woman has determined life for many African-American Muslim women for decades, though not all have accommodated this notion its entirety.

In the last decade, I have been asked the question, "Why Islam?" hundreds of times. It seems to me that the attraction of Islam for women, especially African-American women, is best summarized by Leila Ahmed, who informs us that

> even as Islam instituted, in the initiatory society, a hierarchical structure as the basis of relations between men and women, it also preached, in its

> ethical voice . . . the moral and spiritual equality of all human beings. [21]
>
> It is because Muslim women hear this egalitarian voice that they often declare (generally to the astonishment of non-Muslims) that Islam is non-sexist. [22]

African-American women come to Islam from various educational, social, and economic positions, and their reasons for choosing Islam reflect that diversity. How they lived their previous lives is important for understanding their accommodations and struggles in Islam. Some women, with college educations and opportunities for self-empowerment, come to Islam after the study of several worldviews and/or participation in other traditions. The following remarks from interviews express some of the paths traveled by African-American women toward their encounter with Islam:

> One thing is clear. Christianity is one of the roots of black folk's problems in this country. It's got black folk thinkin' that white folk are God. As long as black folk are singin' and shoutin' in church thinkin' that some White god is gonna save them they will not and can never fight to preserve their humanity. Jesse Jackson tells everybody to say, "I am somebody"—hell, the White man already knows we are somebody. That's why he is kickin' our asses on every level he can.
>
> — *Ayesha*
>
> Everywhere I read there was some mention of Islam or Muslims. I figured I should check it out; this was

very different, wide enough for everybody. More like one huge culture with little communities. God, I already knew about, Muhammad was new but since nobody was worshippin' him he was no problem. Most of all the Qur'an didn't ask me to love those who did evil. This was cool.

—*Sayeeda*

I remember reading Carlos Castaneda and trying to understand the opening of the universe in the mind with the mind-altering drugs. I was too scared to take anything, though, but I got a great imagination and it was working overtime. What was clear though was a different connection with nature and the universe than what I was being taught in school. What some people thought should result in "love," I kinda got the feeling that we have a responsibility to nature.

—*Fareeda*

After spending all my childhood and some of my adult years in Catholicism I knew that what Scriptures say and what people do don't always go together. Islam seemed to be a way for me to be religious just between me and God. There was the stress on community but my personal connection with God didn't depend on anybody else. You know what I mean—there was no confession: God knows and expects me to straighten it out.

—*Maryam*

Other women come to Islam through direct contact with Muslims. Several women talked about meeting Muslim women in public places. They were most aware of the difference in attitude.

> I was in the welfare office talkin' to this sister and she was tellin' me wasn't no sense in gettin' mad with these people 'cause all this was just a moment. People who treated other people like this weren't long for this earth. She said it like it was understood and she knew somethin' deep.
>
> —*Fatimah*

Muslim men also play a role in attracting women to Islam. Muslim men, both immigrant and African-American, engage in African-American women in conversations about Islam and Muslim women. Often the end result of these conversations is a move into Islam.

> I guess I kinda raised myself. They thought I was bright and pretty so if I kept quiet nobody paid me much attention. I liked high school but I just didn't fit—too light to be black and too black to be white. I read all the time—black literature, history, autobiography. My family only paid attention to the fact that I read, wasn't in trouble, and was cute. I wanted to be a doctor—family doctor. So when at fifteen I met this Muslim brother who was about thirty, good-looking, and smart. I listened to what he had to say because he listened to what I had to say and didn't treat me like a kid. He was attentive and Islam was exotic.
>
> —*Sandra*

Further reflections on their lives reveals considerations of life in America.

> College taught the history, philosophy, and literature of Europeans. We learned how primitive, undeveloped, and backward Africans and other people of color were.
>
> —*Ameena*

> Even though my folks walked picket lines and experienced white folks calling them dirty names, throwin' things at them, puttin' their dogs on 'em, they still felt they had to prove they were human. They feel that if they act like white folks they will be accepted by white folks. So they make sure their English is proper. The things we were taught to want and need were European. My folks thought that the key to equality was to be jus' like 'em. They never thought that they were o.k. jus' bein' who they are.
>
> —*Rabiyyah*

> Welfare means you are totally unable to care for yourself, your children. The person on welfare is made to be nobody and is kept in the system by force. I will clean toilets, anything, before I go on welfare and if there is nothing out there to do, I will make stuff and sell it. . . . I know that this country has put a system into motion that feeds on poor people and rather than educate them to be independent of it, it makes more dependencies. It

> constantly penalizes people who try to get out of it so that it can stay alive.
>
> —*Joan*

> In Catholic school, the black children always know that they are different because the priests and nuns tell you in so many ways. They always assume that you are in the special lunch program or that you can't participate in something because of money, they don't ask. When it comes to things like band or the orchestra black kids don't get to go because they are always assigned to gym or sports. Everybody thinks that all black people can do is play games. If you are smart it's unique 'cause black folks aren't supposed to know anything either. In class, the teachers are always cutting you off before you're finished or interpreting what you mean like you can't say what you mean. . . . My mother taught us that any kind of work is work. I might think that I'm too educated for certain types of work by if the alternative is welfare, then to the toilets
>
> —*Leila*

As mentioned in previous chapters, the move into Islam—affirming the *shahadah*—is accompanied by a move into a community. These two levels of contract—one with God and the other with community—are reflected in spirituality and personal space transformation. On the spiritual level, the move into Islam demands a level of consciousness of God—an awareness of *deen* (religion). The God-centeredness of Islam and *wa'ezudeeni Islamiyyah* (Islamic consciousness) are instilled by the performance of *salat*, reading the *Qur'an*, and the use of everyday phrases such as *al-hamdullilah, insha Allah, as-salaamu alaikum, ma'shallah*, and so on. African-American Muslim women describe this God-consciousness in a number of ways. For example, *sawm* (fasting) clears one's sight and tunes one's hearing to one's environment. The discipline of the fast from sunrise to sunset for thirty days while working (in or outside of the home) or attending school, and residing in a culture where the fast has no meaning is one space of spiritual nourishment.

> During Ramadan, I see things differently. It is as though everyone has to be their real selves. People, the people I work with can pretend all the other months of the year except Ramadan. I can see right through them and see who they really are. Ramadan always shocks me with the evil I can see clearly.
>
> —*Rasheeda*

> As I am just talking now I use *inshallah* all the time. Using it makes me remember that nothing I can plan can happen without God's will.
>
> —*Ameena*

> In Islam, my soul has a focus. I know that there is no one who can save me. I must obey God and wait until the last day to see what I have really done in this life. So I try and sometimes fail to keep this on my mind. I pray to stay on the path.
>
> —*Deborah*

> Listening to the Qur'an on tape is something I do everyday. The recitation always brings tears and moves my heart. I don't see how anyone could hear the Qur'an and not be moved. I am learning a new surah a month. When I get to the long ones I guess it will take years, but I will get it done.
>
> —*Bahirah*

In addition to personal spiritual strivings, women also participate in classes and less formal groups for Qur'anic and Arabic studies. These sessions generally are focused on some portion of the *Qur'an* chosen for study and comment on what God intends to be learned from it. Here women seek interpretation from each other using hadith literature and each other's knowledge. Women have little or no opportunity to share their knowledge with the men, but often continue in these sessions for years. One group in Chicago, called Bushra, has had ongoing meetings for fifteen consecutive years. Women's groups have expanded in the past ten years out of local communities to regional organizations, but a major focus remains spirituality.

While women have nurtured their own spirituality, both personally and in groups, the move into Islam on the community level has its own indoctrination. The following remarks indicate some of the difficulties encountered in this indoctrination.

> Befo' I could ketch my breath, they were telling me about all the layers of clothes I had to wear so nobody could lust after me.
>
> —*Hassannah*

> I literally cried when I was told I couldn't listen to my music because it was vulgar. But I refused to get rid of the records. I just had to look at all

those memories. Some sisters "snatched" down pictures of my family off the walls and I freaked out!

—Aisha

I had to learn to go to bed early in order to make the morning prayer and learn the prayer at the same time in Arabic. I used to worry if I had memorized it correctly or if I was mispronouncing words. At first I was scared to make prayer at work because everybody had already started acting funny around me so I waited until I got home and then I worried about having missed the prayer. There was so much to learn that I worried all the time. The only time I could relax was when my menstrual cycle was on.

—Latifah

I went to the masjid to look around, went to some of the classes. Most of the sisters were either my age and real kids or women not paying me any attention. I look back on it and wish I had just joined the other teenagers. Instead I decided that I was a black woman and was bright enough to be on my own. When he showed me what the Qur'an said about men being the maintainers and protectors of women and that Muslim men could have four wives, I thought I was mature enough to handle it. When I met his wife she was nice and thought I was there to learn about Muslim

> women, not to marry her husband. Well, I became a co-wife, second wife, pregnant, high school drop out, family outcast, you name it, all before I turned sixteen. The women at the masjid would not talk to me. I figured and my husband told me they were envious so I just studied Islam and Arabic on my own. My life was hell except for reading the Qur'an and prayer.
>
> —*Sharifah*

> People are people no matter what religious community they belong to. Some are there for security, others seeking knowledge and some just 'cause they think it's a happening. You have to decide why you are there if this presents a problem for you and then go with it. We have sisters who were born Muslim and it is the only way of life they know and we have some who are making mistakes with brothers as they try to find out how they want to be Muslims. Some come into Islam trying to make it Christianity and are confused as they find out it isn't. Its hard to be Muslim in America in the center of a weird kind of Christianity mixed up with all kinds of other things.
>
> —*Jamiliah*

What is life like in these Muslim communities for African-American women? According to many Muslim women it is average American life with a spiritual twist. What does this mean? African-American Muslim women experience all the joys and struggles that their African-American and Muslim sisters experience. These women struggle in the culture of the United States, where women of all social classes struggle; in African-American culture, where women are torn between fighting racism and sexism; and finally in a budding Muslim culture that inherited the Muslim world's misrepresentation of gender relations in Islam. They push against three layers of mire, and are making dents. Those women who struggle with sexism and male domination see Muslim women as necessarily in the service of their mates, but not in a diminutive way.

> Muslim women must see themselves as the backbone of the family and society. If their homes are peaceful, their husbands content, their children loved and safe, then their [own] lives can be productive. There are many ways women can influence men without being out there, up front.
>
> —*Maryam*

> It is inherent in the genetic make-up of the black female to seek to satisfy the black male, to help him meet his goals and to demand good treatment from him.
>
> —*Minister Ava Muhammad*[23]

> The woman in Islam's role is very important, because she has the responsibility, as the Mother of Civilization and first teacher, of teaching these good manners to the (her) children, to continue this polite society.
>
> —*Nyasha Muhammad*[24]

In a widely read and discussed article, "Women of the Veil: Islamic Militants Pushing Women Back to an Age of Official

Servitude," two non-Muslim female journalists for the *Atlantic Journal-Constitution* sparked the ire of African-American Muslim women from all over the country. Led by women in Warithudeen Muhammad's communities, these women rejected the claim that Islam degrades women and makes them servants:

> We urge all Muslim women from all over the world—those born in the religion of Islam and those who have converted to it—to speak out and defend their choice [of Islam] in spirit, word, and in action.[25]

African-American Muslim women who struggle against male dominance do so within a framework that does not mimic Western feminism. These women seek valid Qur'anic interpretation. As Mildred El-Amin argues,

> Many Muslims interpret 4:34 to mean devout obedience to the husband; there is no Qur'anic foundation for this interpretation. Devout obedience is due Allah alone; all human beings are subject to error and ignorance.[26]

In contrast to many Muslim societies, African-American Muslim women spend a great deal of time in the *masjid*, organizing educational programs, doing good in community activities, attending classes, and praying. Like the women of the earliest Muslim communities, most African-American Muslim women attend *Jum'ah* prayer when possible. Separation from men is put into effect differently in different communities. All communities provide for the privacy of women. In two communities I visited—Masjid Ar-Raham on Chicago's West side, and the First Cleveland Mosque in Cleveland—the Imams made concerted efforts to give the women a sense of belonging to the *masjid*, and acknowledged that what women contribute is very important. In those communities, where the Imam is elected based on knowledge of the *Qur'an* and *hadith*, women participate in the community selection. Women also participate in the selection of some of the sites for the *masjid*.

African-American Muslim women have tended on the whole to be better acclimated to various sectors of the work force, though less well educated in professional fields, than their Middle Eastern and Southeast Asian sisters. While the government has seriously restricted Muslim women's educational levels in a number of Muslim communities in the world, racism, religious bias, and sexism in the United States have placed an overwhelming burden on Muslim women. The secular nature of American society is often used to force Muslim women out of positions of high visibility. Most African American women find a great deal of bias and hostility directed toward them, no matter what their status or occupation. Many women are forced either to compromise their appearances in order to maintain employment in mainstream professions, or turn to home businesses for income.

Religious discrimination, particularly toward Islam, is widespread in the United States, but this has not prevented large numbers of African American women from turning to Islam as a way of life. Highly visible as "religious artifacts," African American Muslim women in public spaces are the constant objects of hostilities. In contrast, immigrant Muslim women receive either compliments or other positive regard for their difference in the same public spaces. There seems to be some sort of expectations that Muslim women from the Muslim world will look different, while difference in the appearance of African American Muslim women is not accepted.

Among women in various communities there are points of convergence and divergence on any number of issues. In general, African American Muslim women live in a closed society that is highly charged with rumor, innuendo, envy, love, nurturing, and spirituality. These women strive to overcome the negative in search of the positive—most times.

Conclusion

In the course of this study, we have seen that African-American Islamic expressions are numerous, diverse, and sometimes at odds, but are nevertheless growing and maturing into a distinct Muslim culture. We have also seen that African-American Islamic communities have often been misrepresented, that their Islamic interpretations have been heavily influenced by outsiders, and that they have all struggled to find an authentic or at least viable Islamic expression. Rather than stop with these generalizations, let me briefly review what I can see as the evolution of African-American Islamic expressions.

The first Muslim community had a number of obstacles to confront and overcome under the tutelage of the Prophet Muhammad Ibn Abdullah of Mecca, Arabia. Two of those obstacles were a fatalistic world view and a tribalism whose values were totally based upon the achievements of men. Pre-Islamic Arabic culture was settled in tribes whose moral life and other social arrangements were based in an ancestral tradition. It was not that these tribes lacked virtues and values. As one noted Islamic scholar asserts:

> We would be doing gross injustice to the pre-Islamic Arabs if we maintained that there was among them no distinction between right and wrong, between what is good and what is bad. On the contrary, a careful perusal of a document such as the famous "Book of Songs," *Kitab al-Aghani*, will at once convince us that the pagan Arabs were in reality endowed with an acute sense of morality.[1]

Thus, what the Prophet Muhammad offered his tribe was not the ability to distinguish right from wrong, but "the principle of morality" which "had its origin in his glowing belief in the one and only God." The scope of this task is confirmed by the attention given to it in the Meccan suras of the *Qur'an*.

Another aspect of this task was to not only seat the *'asabiya* (tribal solidarity based on similar interests) firmly within a God-originated principle of morality, but also to introduce the notion of *ummah* (the community of believers which transcended tribal difference). For the first community, this radical notion would change the entire social arrangement, by functioning as a dynamic concept that clarified how the tribes were to know one another. (Surprisingly, this important notion has received little scholarly attention.) For most of the history of Muslim cultures, tribalness has not been seen as something to be destroyed, but as an inherent tendency that must be informed by Divine principles of morality and an understanding of the House of Islam which must stand against unbelief. In Islamic history the interpretations of the Qur'anic message and the resultant practices among the various communities (i.e., Egyptian, Turkish, Indian) have grown largely unexamined for their Islamic content. As Islam spread out of the Arabian peninsula, communities that became Muslim retained many of their pre-Islamic practices and societal arrangements, such as female circumcision and the roles of women. In most places these pre-Islamic practices became validated as Islamic practices and have been passed on to generations. The primary obligation of new Muslim communities has largely been allegiance to the caliph and participation in the core acts of worship. When a student reads the history of particular Muslim cultures, as Hasan Al-Turabi says, "all practices and mores are presented as Islamic." The dominant "face" of Islam after the death of Prophet Muhammad ibn Abdullah quickly became a legal one. Those communities and philosophies that rose in resistance to the dominance of legal interpretations of the *Qur'an* and the Sunnah, i.e., those interpretations that asserted the allegorical or symbolic or the ethical to balance the legal, were and still are branded as heretical. These marginalized histories, interpretations, and assertions have generally been masked from general knowledge by the dominant discourse of the law.

We know little about the Islam that came to the shores of America in the hearts and practices of Muslim slaves, primarily because of another masking discourse, i.e. that of Christianity and the institution of slavery. What we do know is that in twentieth-century America, African-American ex-slaves rediscover and reassert Islam as a worldview. The dominant forces of Christianity and racism immediately move to marginalize any Islamic presence. For mainstream society the natural inclination for one particular human community—African-American—towards *'asabiya* is a position that cannot be permitted. Why? Perhaps because when a community understands what social solidarity can mean, they can never be slaves. In this early environment, a new assertion of *ummah* also presents itself. This assertion, packed in the bags of immigrant Muslims, has been molded in response to racism, colonialism, and the need for survival. Survival by most immigrant Muslims has translated into being like white Americans. For African-Americans survival has meant group solidarity, with periodic alliances with powerful communities such as liberal white Christians and Jews.

The history of Islam is not a static history. Rather it encompasses all of those waves of cultural formation that seem to be necessary for the establishment of a civilization that in its expanse is by necessity multicultural, multiethnic, and multilinguistic. Islam has never come to a community and completely erased that community's past or present. When Islam comes to a community, it imprints its core beliefs at a fundamental level and stamps its worldview on the identity of the believer through the practices. The Muslim is tied to an Islamic historical continuum that is universal in nature. African-American Muslims can be clearly seen as tied to this continuum. Most African-Americans understand the notion of a "lost nation" so well developed by the Moorish Science Temple and the Nation of Islam, and most African-American Muslims would consider themselves "found" in Islam, whether the finding be through the teaching of a person or through personal searching resulting in community membership. Scholars researching AfricanAmerican life must also explore the environment surrounding the emergence of political and spiritual movements. This approach acknowledges agency on the part of African-Americans rather than assuming that their lives are only reactions to external stimuli.

African-American Islamic expressions have maintained the Islamic notions of social justice, absolute faith in the one God, and willingness to assert Islam in the face of all odds—even against the American government and its armies. This statement is not absolute, however, as individual African-American Muslim leaders have sometimes lead their communities to survival by inclusion, foreswearing Islamic notions. But the majority of the early communities clearly interpreted their being Muslim as the only priority, followed by the need to organize around a de facto *'asabiya.* They apparently felt more secure in Islam against racism than in any other social arrangement. We may never know how Noble Drew Ali came to Islam. There is no documented story about Ali's introduction to Islam, even though there are stories about his presence in the court of the Queen of England, where he was allegedly awarded the title, Noble. He then reported went to Arabia to the court of King Ibn Saud who, community members believe, gave him permission to write the *Circle Seven Koran*. Researchers on this community have found no documented evidence of these events. Whatever the origin of his Islamic expression, Noble Drew Ali's simple assertion that a person must have a nationality led many to his doors. Elijah Muhammad, on the other hand, had a documented beginning with Islam through Noble Drew Ali and W. Fard Muhammad. Discrepancies arise as to what this man's name really was, where he was from, and even if he was really Muslim, but that he had knowledge of Islam was undisputed. That the Nation of Islam is a committed group of believers in a community that continues to grow is also documentable. The initial encounters of other early community leaders with Islam, though undocumented, were evidently through meetings with Noble Drew Ali, Elijah Muhammad, or Muslims who had immigrated.

For African-Americans, the viability of Islam as a worldview hinged largely on its primary emphasis on social justice, and its ability to provide African-Americans with an historical identity independent of slavery. Noble Drew Ali endeavored and succeeded in giving his community an identifiable history, a worldview that provided God-ordained principles of morality, and a physical place of ancestry. For an ex-slave population, this provided important social and spiritual support. One could argue that the notion of prophethood ascribed to Ali was part of the general climate of evangelical Protestant Christianity—or one could say that anyone who did the things he did deserved the title. An examination of the social landscape of the time reveals an America brewing with ethnic groups proud of their heritages. Having been deprived of the major aspects of culture, African-Africans struggled to establish themselves in all their diversity as a people, to fight racism and its violence, and to decide the nature of their relationship with their former legal masters. This was an enormous task, since many whites still acted in accordance with the Dred Scott decision of 1857, which asserted that "the fundamental question facing the Court . . . was whether Scott as a black could become part of the people." The answer of Chief Justice Taney to this question was clear:

African American Islam

> They [the blacks] had for more than a century before [the Revolution] been regarded as beings of an inferior order, and altogether unfit to associate with the white race, either in social or political relations; and so far inferior, that they had no rights which the white man was bound to respect; and that the negro might justly and lawfully be reduced to slavery for his benefit. He was bought and sold, and treated as an ordinary article of merchandise and traffic, whenever a profit could be made by it.[2]

In the first decades of the twentieth century, Americans of African descent lived their lives under legal segregation, and were denied voting rights and the right to life. The need to establish a viable culture was clear. In this context, Islam provided African-Americans with a worldview that contained notions of God's Will and a complete "self-help" program. The Muslim's faith depends solely on his efforts—there are no intercessors. Islam demands that the Muslim stand for what is right and forbid, uncompromisingly, what is wrong. It commands that the Muslim act as a believer on all occasions and that he/she not rest until there is social justice. The leaders of the first African-American Muslim communities all promote an unyielding Islam. The enemy is identified, the lack of social justice is targeted, and the need to organize the community against any obstacle is emphasized.

With as little as fifty years of a concrete Islamic presence, the communities in the second half of the twentieth century show the full range of possible historical Islamic expressions. There are those with special messengers and prophets—the Moorish Science Temple, three distinct Nations of Islam, the Ahmadiyyah Movement in Islam, the Nation of Gods and Earths—as well as those organized around specific legal philosophies—Darul Islam, the Islamic Party, Jamil Al-Amin's communities, the First Pittsburgh Mosque, the Islamic Mission to America, and the Ansaruallah. There are also those whose continuing evolution in Islamic thought is toward an American Muslim school of thought—such as Warithudeen Muhammad's communities—and those who have grasped the more ethical and spiritual dimensions of Islam—in tariqa such as Naqshabandiyyah and Tijaniyyah.

As I have emphasized throughout this work, the tension between *'asabiya* and *ummah* is a persistent issue for contemporary communities. Many communities have kept their nation-building focus and minimized their contact with the *ummah*. As knowledge of the Muslim world grows, encounters with paternalism and racism grow. One hallmark of Muslim community in the contemporary world is its claim to uphold the Qur'anic exhortation to the brotherhood of believers and the equality of the believers before Allah, with piety as the only distinguishing mark of superiority.

Diversity and multiculturalism have always been a part of Islam. While Muslims have always existed as ethnic groups, they have always fought assumptions of ethnic superiority. Saudi Arabs have asserted claims of superiority because they are the guardians of the Ka'aba. Some Arabs have sought to align countries based on their Arab ethnic solidarity. The list could go on and on. The major education centers in Saudi Arabia and Egypt have housed the best potential scholars from the Muslim world; colonialism has made sure that race is an issue that abounds in each society, as black African Muslims can attest. In America, where these nationals are in a kind of Muslim melting pot, the tensions are heightened.

There has emerged a distinct division between the Pakistani, the Indian, Arabian, and African-American communities which can be seen clearly in publications, organizational structures, and at social gatherings. The predominant group of native-born Muslims, African-Americans, is rarely if ever consulted in *da'wah* efforts. The impression is made that Islam only comes with the successive waves of Muslim immigrants. This division is also observable in the lack of partnerships between immigrants and African-Americans. It has also been postulated that, for immigrants, there is a monolithic

Islam in the Muslim world which is normative and the real experiences of African-American Muslims should be rejected; instead they should aspire to effect something called "orthodox" Islam. This assertion continues in some quarters of the Muslim community as a stimulus to divisiveness. Yet as non-Muslim writers from the West uncover the experiences of Muslims in the Muslim world and all their expressions, African-American Muslims see that their expressions and reactions to living in America have currency, precedence, and counterparts in the history and traditions of Islam. Conversely, the behavior of some members of the immigrant community is seen by African-Americans as having its counterpart: the behavior of imperialists and colonizers. The distressing aspect of that observation is that, in America, one is free to express deeply felt feelings and opinions, especially those which emerge out of a deeply ingrained worldview. Yet, in this context, immigrant Muslims are observed simultaneously expressing an idealized and romanticized Islam. And it is an Islam which belies the slide of some Muslim communities into tribalism, social apathy, and paralysis. Interactions are strained between African American Muslim communities, between African American and immigrant communities, and between the general Islamic presence and American Christianity and Judaism. These layers of tension have not evolved into unrestrained hostilities, but have increased significantly despite efforts by some communities for dialogue. The feelings on the part of many African American Muslims is that the Dred Scott Decision is still in effect, and is affecting relations between their communities and other groups.

In addition to these general tensions, contemporary African-American Muslims are confronted with mounting concerns about family, the law, education, and the workplace. Muslims are beginning to feel the tensions present in the general society, but have not organized themselves to make an impact. For the most part the communities have been insular, without participation in society on any large scale. The one exception to this is the Nation of Islam under Louis Farrakhan. This is the first community to participate in any meaningful way in an AIDS project, and one of only a few to provide security for areas plagued with crime and drugs. Family disintegration is also beginning to affect Muslims at almost the same rate as in the general population. The added effects of polygyny, and a suspiciousness towards the courts with regard to alimony and child custody in Muslim communities, are just beginning to break into the open.

Since the immigrant communities prefer to keep their private schools separate, African American Muslims are struggling to build schools and keep them running and to find qualified teachers. Efforts in this area are expanding, and there are some notable schools in Atlanta and Los Angeles. As the education crisis escalates, Muslims are turning to overseas options and home schooling. The issue of the law is an ongoing problem in the general African-American community and affects Muslims proportionately. Muslim communities have not set up halfway houses to assist in the rehabilitation of Muslim ex-prisoners, nor have the communities provided any sustained instruction for inmates (with the exception of the Nation of Islam and a small community in New York).

The issues of the workplace and politics are frequently discussed. Some communities eschew any collaboration with the political machine of America, and thus forego the possibility of the kind of participation that would permit lobbying for holidays and recognition as a potential mass of voters. But politicians have not let their numbers go uncounted and have made efforts to convince some communities otherwise. As African American Muslims continue to champion the rights of Muslims overseas, perhaps some of the negative attitudes about the political system will change. On the other hand, reporting in the media that encourages anti-Muslim sentiments may bring about the opposite result.

While I know that the reader is waiting for some concluding remarks about Muslim women, I will instead take the opportunity to open a conversation on the status of Muslim men. (Since the topic is always Muslim women, I decided to give the men a chance.) Many of the Muslim men I spoke to about community, the workplace, education, and family had a lot to say. They see a struggle to establish Islam in this country. While they know that Muslims are encouraged to emigrate to Muslim lands, they also know that there is no garden there either. They were torn over many important issues. They did not want to "sell" Islam down the drain in the attempt to make Islam palatable to Christian America or to the Jewish community. What they did seem to suggest was relationships of respect and cooperation with other groups on issues that negatively affected the whole of America—such as gangs, drugs, and violence.

Many men are quite upset at the paternalistic attitudes of foreign Muslims, and had resolved to keep their relationships with them on a "prayer level." They also appeared agitated that racism had been exported everywhere, and in such ways that they had no control over how African American Islam was represented. The men I talked to were just as upset over the way they were being depicted as oppressors of women. These men asserted that some women had choices that they did not exercise, while others were oppressed and complicitous in the situation. Leaders in some communities were adamant about eradicating any oppression of women, and had begun to talk about the situation in the Friday *Khutbah*.

When asked about the future of the Muslim community, all of the men expressed a desire for unity among the Muslims, a sigh at the apparent lack of a significantly supported leadership, and a heartfelt commitment to making an American Islam. The issues around unity are complex because of the diversity, but the men seemed intent upon finding ways—or I should say events—around which they can open dialogue. Leadership has the same problems because of the diversity of thought. Imams Jamil Al-Amin and Warithudeen Muhammad have some support, but not nearly enough for one to emerge clearly as a spokesman for all of African American Islam. The Honorable Louis Farrakhan is still in the process of evolution with regard to Islam, and while he is surely the most outspoken voice for the sentiments of many African Americans and African American Muslims, he is not the generally recognized spokesman that many Americans take him to be. Where and if one spokesman emerges will only be determined by future events.

Conclusion

In closing, I would like to emphasize that the amount of research that could be done any one of the communities examined in this text is enormous, as is the research that could go forward on their positions in Islamic history. My intention, again, is to open a conversation and, *inshallah*, I have done that.

Appendices

The following materials on the "Purposes and Objectives" of the Midwest Muslim Women's Association and the "Conditions of Bas'at" in the Ahmadiyyat Movement in Islam supplement discussions in previous chapters, and are intended to provide the reader with a further glimpse into comtemporary Islamic life in America.

Actual Facts

The total area of the land and water of the Planet Earth is 196,940,000 square miles.

The circumference of the Planet Earth is 24,896 miles.

The diameter of the Earth is 7,926 miles.

The area of the Land is 57,255,000 square miles.

The area of the Water is 139,685,000 square miles.

The Pacific Ocean covers 68,634,000 square miles.

The Atlantic Ocean covers 41,321,000 square miles.

The Indian Ocean covers 29,430,000 square miles.

The Lakes and Rivers cover 1,000,000 square miles.

The Hills and Mountains cover 14,000,000 square miles.

The Islands are 1,910,000 square miles.

The Deserts are 4,861,000 square miles.

Mount Everest is 29,141 feet high.

The Producing Land is 29,000,000 square miles.

The Earth weighs six sextillion tons—(a unit followed by 21 ciphers)

The Earth is 93,000,000 ;miles from the Sun.

The Earth travels at the rate of 1,037 1/3 miles per hour.

Light travels at the rate of 186,000 miles per second.

Sound travels through air at the rate of 1,120 feet per second.

The diameter of the Sun is 853,000 miles.

THE DECLARATION OF THE FEDERATION OF MUSLIM COMMUNITIES

1. We, the Islamic people of The Federation of Muslim Communities, declare that there is nothing worthy of worship except Allah and that Prophet Muhammad is indeed Allah's final Prophet for mankind and our blessed leader.

2. We declare that we represent no sect nor division in Islam; rather, we are Muslims following only Islam as expressed in the Holy Qur'an and in the action of Holy Prophet Muhammad. Also, we listen to and have great respect for all the good and correct contributions of all the great Imams, both past and present.

3. We declare that the only purpose of our Federation is to serve Allah, teach His religion and establish ourselves according to His will.

4. We decare that we will guide our Federation by the Holy Qur'an and Sunnah of our Prophet, only.

5. We declare that for this Federation, all power of authority and law rests with Allah. In those areas of legislation where Allah allows us to use our reasoning, we will not institute any laws that disagree with or contravene any of the dictates of Holy Qur'an and/or way of Holy Prophet.

6. We declare that in order to help facilitate our coordination and unity, we will always elect one from among us who will be our Imam. An Imam will remain our representative as long as the Majlis Shura of the Federation agree that he should. The Majlis Shura (Executive Council) shall consist of the Imams of each affiliate community.

7. We declare that each and every adult Muslim of this Federation has the right to express himself on any aspect of his Federation.

Signed originally by:

Imam Dawud ibn Ahmad Salahuddin
Al-Jamaat Al-Muslimoon, Chicago, Ill.

Iman Yusuf Muzaffaruddin Hamid
Masjid-Ul-Ummah, Washington, D.C.

Amir Abdur-Rahim Shaheed
The Islamic Center, Pittsburgh, Pa.

Date: Zul-Qi'dah 14, 1391
January 1, 1972

YUSUF MUZAFFARUDIN HAMID
IMAM
AND BOARD CHAIRMAN OF
COMMUNITY MOSQUE, INC.

MASJID UL-UMMAH
THE COMMUNITY MOSQUE

14 Sha'ban 1390

Dear Brother:

By the Mercy of Allah, the movement for Islamic renewal and revival is creating a mighty response throughout the American continent as well as the world. Masjid ul-Ummah is an active participant in this Islamic cause and has been successful in assuming a useful role of suggestion, support, and assistance to the Islamic community in America. A few months ago, the Imam of our Community Mosque had occasion to set forth in detail the aims and objectives that guide our work. There are presented below.

AMIR OF INFORMATION

CLARIFICATION OF GOALS AND OBJECTIVES

I. OBJECTIVES

A. To bring about conscious Muslims: Muslims comprising a community of people who serve Allah willingly after deciding that His Way is the only way.
B. To have their hands joined with all Muslim hands in order to bring about an Islamic State.

II. MASJID UL-UMMAH

A. The mosque serves to create a base of operations for foundations of an Islamic Community.
B. *Ahl ul-Islam* (The Islamic People) means those men, women, children, families, of young and old, etc., who believe in the *Kalima* of Islam: The Muslims.

C. Masjid ul-Ummah will create mechanisms to start serving the needs of their people in an Islamic fashion.

(1) Administration

a. The Imam functions with an Amirate which is compromised of practical branches, such as: Amir of Health and Welfare, Amir of Information, Amir of Finance, and as the need develops, Amir of Defense and Amir of Education, which branches are directl)y under the Imam's guidance.

b. The Amirate, from its direct contact with the Community and from consultation with the Imam, must be creative in bringing about the programs to serve the practical needs of the Community.

c. The Amirate should be the mechanism for redressing the grievances of the masses and for keeping them progressive.

d. The Majlis Shura (Advisory Council to the Imam) means those elected representatives of the Community whose main purpose is to act as an advisory council to all major community policy decisions of the Imam, and whenever he feels it necessary to convene it. The Majlis Shura may also act as the Community court bench with the Imam, until establishment of a judiciary within the Community.

(2) Creation of a force of Brothers instrumental in spreading Islam and widening Community frontiers (*Ikhwan ul-Islamiyun*).

a. The *Ikhwan ul-Islamiyun* is the *fard kifaya* of the general community (*Ahl ul-Islam*).

b. *Ikhawan ul-Islamiyun* represents those brothers in the general community who sacrifice the time and energy deemed necessary to see to it that *Ahl ul-Islam* always remain on a progressive Islamic frame.

c. Bringing about the *Ikhwan ul-Islamiyun* is the most difficult aspect of community development, representing the Force of Islam, the Islamic Movement.

III. ISLAMIC MOVEMENT

A. An Islamic Movement is built by long and patient development; it is not a spontaneous thing.

B. "The Arabs of the desert say they have believed..." (49:14) *Ahl ul-Islam* have submitted, but as a whole they are not ready to make the necessary sacrifices to become *Ikhwan ul-Islamiyan.*

(1) To bring about *Ikhwan ul-Islamiyan.* the simplicity of Islam should be stressed.

a. It must be shown that the Holy Prophet (PBUH) always spoke in a simple way; he never used highly philosophical phrases.

b. The masses should not be carried so deeply into Islam philosophically, so as to become confused.

(2) The Ikhwan must have special educational training, but distinguished from mere intellectual studies.

a. They must have similar material for group studies.

b. They must couple their practical field work with their studies.

c. They must understand that change does not come from intellectuals sitting in chairs with books in hand, though they must understand the necessity for the book and how and when to use it, because not only was the Prophet (PBUH) unlettered according to the standard of his day, but the first revelation was "Iqraa!"

d. They must always try to keep theoretical and practical things apart.

e. They must live a full, active, responsible life in all fields.

f. It is important to concentrate on the many problems of living in the U.S. in the light of Qur'an and Sunnah, for we must be able to show Muslims in the U.S. how to live in the U.S. and at the same time maintain a good Muslim life.

g. There must be simple beginnings. A well-organized, disciplined group can grow with time into a powerful force.

h. They must establish practical relations with all Islamic forces and organizations in the world, be they national or international.

IV. MEANS

A. With respect to finances, the Community wants to exist primarily from the sacrifices of the individuals concerned.

B. We must avail ourselves of any Islamic assistance that can be received from a no-strings-attached source, national or international.

C. We can project establishment of bookstores and other Community businesses.

D. The character of the Community must be molded by the Qur'an; it should house everything the Qur'an has allowed and approved.

(1) It must be concerned with basic ibadat, moral ity, education, the family system, means of liveli hood, etc.

(2) Its whole tenor should be Islamic, without lop-sided specialization in just certain disciplines causing the Community to assume the character of an army, or group of saints, or political activists.

(3) Masjid ul-Ummah is not on the defensive with an objective of stopping all un-Islamic groups; its objective is to positively work for Islam and to deal with any opposition as it arises, and as the circumstances require.

E. The character of the Community must not be reactionary. It must be able to speak objectively and work for Islam, dealing with the negatives as they arise.

F. The Community must shun isolationism and recognize the necessity of international contacts and the benefits deriving therefrom, such as migration, *hajj*, special training in Islamic disciplines, protection from un-Islamic forces, current literature on international Islamic affairs.

V. INVOLVEMENT IN THE OUTER (NON-MUSLIM) COMMUNITY

A. The purpose of projects directed to the outer community as this stage of development should be to awaken awareness of Islam there, by purely Islamic methods and without overextending ourselves.

B. The primary concern now is to strengthen our own ranks. For the information of the outer community there are various projects such as the Sunday lectures (Islam in Africa, The Islamic Process of Revolution, Islam and Slavery, etc.) which hit on the core needs of this community, book projects and College campus lectures.

C. Our efforts must go proportionately and with a full view of our immediate priorities.

VI. CORPORATION

A. The incorporated entity, The Community Mosque, Inc., serves as a legal mechanism that can be used by the Community to further the objectives of the Community in specific areas that are not in themselves un-Islamic, such as:

(1) Acquiring property. With this mechanism, property can be acquired.

(2) The tax-exempted status means saving money.

(3) The corporation can be used as a legal mechanism to bring about the establishment of Islamic schools, hospitals, etc.

VII. TACTICS

We live in an age of *Jahiliyah* and immorality comparable to that of 7th century Arabia.We have no better example of proper tactics for Community development than that provided by our Holy Prophet. He was firm, consistent, and patient, but he did not begin immediately to take on all the politicians and governments of the unbelievers. He established a core of knowledgeable, dedicated, quality-conscious believers whose faith was tested through many trials and ordeals. The early emphasis of the Holy Prophet was on Muslim education and personal sacrifice for the cause of Allah. He did not start out with a band of political revolutionaries. After the Muslim Ummah became strong and powerful as a result of following the Straight Way of Allah, and being built first upon a strong educational and moral foundation, Allah Almighty blessed them with victory on the political and social level as well. We, therefore, emphasize the quality-conscious methodology of the Holy Prophet.

SUMMARY

"The guidance of Allah is the only guidance." (II: 120). The Islamic Community can progress and develop and produce Brothers who exemplify the Force of Islam only by following the Way of Allah as outlined in the Holy Qur'an and in the life of His Holy Prophet (PBUH). Any other approaches, even if they appear for a time to be successful, and however rational, are man-made and will not receive the blessings of Allah. We are safe only in the hand of Allah and there is no Wisdom greater than His. Islam is His religion and the duty of Muslims is not to direct Allah, but to submit to the Way He has outlined for getting things done. If we do not submit to the guidance of Allah we will surely be of those who go astray.

IMAM
17 safar 1390

Conditions of Bai'at (Initiation)
Ahmadiyya Movement in Islam

By

Hazarat Mirza Ghulam Ahmad of Qadian
The Promised Messiah and Mahdi (peace be upon him)

I. The initiate shall solemnly promise that he/she shall abstain from *Shirk* (association of any partner with God) right up to the day of his/her death.

II. That he/she shall keep away from falsehood, fornication, adultery, tresspasses of the eye, debauchery, dissipation, cruelty, dishonesty, mischief and rebellion; and will not permit himself/herself to be carried away by passions, however strong they may be.

III. That he/she shall regularly offer the five daily prayers in accordance with the commandments of God and the Holy Prophet; and shall try his/her best to be regular in offering the *Tahajjud* (pre-dawn supererogatory prayers) and invoking *Darood* (blessings) on the Holy Prophet; that he/she shall make it his/her daily routine to ask forgiveness for his/her sins, to remember the bounties of god and to praise and glorify Him.

IV. That under the impulse of any passions, he/she shall cause no harm whatsoever to the creatures of Allah in general, and Muslims in particular, neither by his/her tongue nor by his/her hands not by any other means.

V. That he/she shall remain faithful to God in all circumstances of life, in sorrow and happiness, adversity and prosperity, in felicity and trials; and shall in all conditions remain resigned to the decree of Allah and keep himself/herself ready to face all kinds of indignities and sufferings in His way and shall never turn away from it at the onslaught of any misfortune; on the contrary, he/she shall march forward.

VI. That he/she shall refrain from following un-Islamic customs and lustful inclinations, and shall completely submit himself/herself to the authority of the Holy Quaran [sic];

and shall make the Word of God and the Sayings of the Holy Prophet the guiding principles in every walk of his/her life.

VII. That he/she shall entirely give up pride and vanity and shall pass all hsi/her in lowliness, humbleness, cheerfulness, forbearance and meekness.

VIII. That he/she shall hold faith, the honor of faith, and the cause of Islam dearer to him/her than his/her life, wealth, honor, children and all other dear ones.

IX. That he/she shall keep himself/herself occupied in the service of God's creatures, for His sake only; and shall endeavor to benefit mankind to the best of his/her Godgiven abilities and powers.

X. That he/she shall enter into a bond of brotherhood with this humble servant of God, pledging obedience to me in everything good, for the sake of Allah, and remain faithful to it till the day of his/her death; that he/she shall exert such a high devotion in the observance of this bond as is not to be found in any other worldly relationship and connections demanding devoted dutifulness.

—Translation from *Isherhar Takmeel-e-Tabligh*, 12 January 1889

بسم الله الرحمن الرحيم

INITIATION FORM

Hazrat Amerul Momineen Mirza Tahir Ahmad
Khalifatul Masih IV
(May Allah strengthen your hand)

Assalamu Alaikum Wa Rahmatullahe Wa Barakatuhoo

I have studied and I wholeheartedly accept the "Conditions of Bai'at (Initiation). "hereby submit the following initiation form, duly completed, and request Huzoor to kindly accept my pledge of initiation.

أَشْهَدُ أَنْ لَّا إِلٰهَ إِلَّا اللّٰهُ وَحْدَهُ لَا شَرِيْكَ لَهُ وَأَشْهَدُ أَنَّ مُحَمَّدًا عَبْدُهُ وَرَسُوْلُهُ

I bear witness that Allah alone is to be worshipped. He is One having no partner, and I bear witness that Muhammad is the Servant and Messenger of Allah

أَشْهَدُ أَنْ لَّا إِلٰهَ إِلَّا اللّٰهُ وَحْدَهُ لَا شَرِيْكَ لَهُ وَأَشْهَدُ أَنَّ مُحَمَّدًا عَبْدُهُ وَرَسُوْلُهُ

I bear witness that Allah alone is to be worshipped. He is One having no partner, and I bear witness that Muhammad is the Servant and Messenger of Allah

أَسْتَغْفِرُ اللّٰهَ رَبِّيْ مِنْ كُلِّ ذَنْبٍ وَأَتُوْبُ إِلَيْهِ

I hereby pledge my initiation at the hand of Hazrat Mirza Tahir Ahmad and enter the Ahmadiyya Movement in Islam. I seek forgiveness from Allah of all my past sins and will do my utmost to guard myself against all kinds of sins in future. I will not associate anyone with Allah. I will not entertain ill will. I will not indulge in backbiting. I will not cause sufferings to anyone. I will give precedence to my faith over all wordly objects. I will constantly endeavour to abide by all the Commands of Islam. I will try my utmost ot read, listen to, recite and narrate the Holy Quran, Sayings of the Holy Prophet (may peace and blessings of Allah be upon him) and the books of the Promised Messiah (peace be on him). I will obey you in everything good that you will tell me. I will always have firm faith in the Holy Prophet Muhammad (peace and blessings of Allah be upon him) as Khatamun Nabiyyeen—the Seal of the Prophets, and will believe in all the claims of the Promised Messiah (on him be peace).

أَسْتَغْفِرُ اللهَ رَبِّيْ مِنْ كُلِّ ذَنْبٍ وَّأَتُوْبُ إِلَيْهِ

I beg pardon from Allah, my Lord, from all my sins and turn to Him.

أَسْتَغْفِرُ اللهَ رَبِّيْ مِنْ كُلِّ ذَنْبٍ وَّأَتُوْبُ إِلَيْهِ

I beg pardon from Allah, my Lord, from all my sins and turn to Him.

أَسْتَغْفِرُ اللهَ رَبِّيْ مِنْ كُلِّ ذَنْبٍ وَّأَتُوْبُ إِلَيْهِ

I beg pardon from Allah, my Lord, from all my sins and turn to Him.

رَبِّ إِنِّيْ ظَلَمْتُ نَفْسِيْ وَاعْتَرَفْتُ بِذَنْبِيْ فَاغْفِرْ لِيْ ذُنُوْبِيْ فَإِنَّهُ لَا يَغْفِرُ الذُّنُوْبَ إِلَّا أَنْتَ

O my Lord, My Allah, I wronged my soul and I confess all my sins; pray forgive my sins, for there is none else except Thee to forgive. Ameen!

Midwest Muslim Women's Association

Purpose and Objectives

1448 East 52nd Street, Suite 204
Chicago, IL 60615

PURPOSE

The purpose of the organization shall be to exemplify the model women in this society based on the Holy Qur'an and the Sunnah of Prophet Muhammad (pbuh). To address the concerns of Muslim women by providing a local, state, and regional platform for sharing information, leadership skills, and resources. To build a comprehensive state and regional network for Muslim women and to conduct conferences and seminars governing issues of concern for Muslim women in America. NOTE: The concerns of Muslim women should be the concerns of all right-minded women. The organizational leadership should consist of Muslim women, but the organization is open to all women.

OBJECTIVES

We accept Allah as the sole sovereign of our bodies, our minds, our souls, our lives, and of the universe. Our objectives are:

1. To be guided by the Qur'an and Hadith of the Prophet Muhammad (pbuh) in all our efforts.

2. To exist from the outset and thereafter as an independent organization and not as a subgrouping of any other organization, group, or body whether on this continent or elsewhere.

3. To be committed to the belief in and practice of basic equality among all human beings.

4. To acknowledge and support elements and practices of North American society compatible with Islamic values.

5. To cooperate with individuals, organizations, institutions, etc.

6. To focus primarily on Muslim females in North America and their needs.

7. To work for the preservation of the basic human rights and dignity of Muslim females and all others.

8. To help Muslim females realize their full potential.

9. To review and research all Islamic "knowledge" concerning Muslim women's identity, rights, and responsibilities.

10. To improve the knowledge of Muslim females in all areas of their lives.

11. To be mutually supportive of each other in our family and work roles.

12. To celebrate the advances of each one of us as an additive to all.

13. To identify and utilize Muslim female expertise.

14. To teach and encourage the practice of female-male relations based on the Qur'an and Hadith.

Glossary of Terms

Adab Discipline of the mind and good qualities of mind and soul. Good manners, politeness.

Afrocentricity The worldview from the perspective of the culture, beliefs, and tradition of the "African" culture.

Allah The Arabic name for the Supreme Being.

Akeeka The ceremony of naming a baby, clipping its hair seven days after the Muslim child's birth.

'Asabiya "Solidarity," "group feeling," "group consciousness." A party or company of traditionally ten to forty men who league together to defend one another against hostile conduct.

Bai'at A pledge of allegiance to a Muslim leader in which the pledgemaker voluntarily and advisedly makes his/her resources, time, finances and talents available to an Islamic leader or sheikh.

Chiliasm Belief in the coming of the millennium (the last thousand years).

Dawah Facilitating people's understanding of Islam by various-means—e.g. example, speech, persuasive argument, practicing *'adab* in one's everyday life, etc.

Darul Harb The world or those societies and governments in the world which are in opposition to Islam. The opposite of Darul Islam.

Deen The religion of El-Islam.

Dhikr "Remembering" God. A form of spiritual discipline.

Dunya The world operating outside of the rules and laws of Islam.

Eid al-Adha Arabic for the commemoration of Prophet Abraham's effort to sacrifice his only son Ismail, in compliance with what he understood the command of Allah to be. During this observance, each adul-Muslim family must "ritually sacrifice" an animal, a chicken, lamb, cow or camel.

Ethnicity The racial and cultural origins of a person or people.

Fasting Refraining from speech, actions and behaviors as proscribed by Allah—e.g., as when Muslims refrain from drink, food, vanity, and intimacy with one's spouse from before sunrise to sunset during the month of Ramadan.

Fatwa A learned legal opinion given by a jurist.

Fiqh The law itself. Islamic jurisprudence based on the Qur'an and the traditions of Muhammad and the wisdom of a jurist.

Ethnicity The racial and cultural origins of a person or a people.

Fasting Holding oneself back from speech actions and behhe Qur'an and the traditions of Muhammad; Jurisprudence.

Hadith "reports" traditions of the Prophet Muhammad which are considered as a source of the Shari'ah, contingent on it's conformity with the Qur'an.

Hadramawt A province or city on the coast of the Arabian peninsula.

Hajj Arabic for the pilgrimage of Muslims to Mecca and its environs.

The Hostage Crisis Refers to the taking of officials of the

American Embassy in Iran as hostages for 444 days beginning in 1979 during President Carter's Administration, by Iranian students, to protest the United States embassy's being used to spy on the country for the apparent purpose of defeating or subverting the Islamic government, in complicity with the Shah of Iran. The specific action of the hostage taking was a response to President Carter's granting of asylum to the Shah of Iran and Carter's later refusal to hand over the Shah to the new government in Iran to answer for human rights violations against the Iranian people.

Imam The leader of Islamic prayers, and in America the leader of the community.

Islam "Submission," "surrender." The Muslim religion; a monotheistic religion in which the supreme deity is Allah and the prophet is Muhammad ibn Abdullah.

Islamic law The Shari'ah; the code of laws and rules governing the life and behavior of Muslims; although not a single book.

Islamic Having the characteristic of the traditions, ritual, and thought of those who call themselves "Muslim."

Islamicity The degree or extent to which a thing, concept, or person exhibits the character or signs of Islam's influence or effect.

Islamicization The rendering of a thing or concept under the influence or with the imprimatur of the Islamic worldview.

Jahiliyyah A time characterized by the supremacy of irrationality and ignorance over revelation and revelation-based reasoning. A term referring to a description of Arabia before the advent of the Prophet Muhammad. Any period of time, before or after the life of Muhammad, so characterized.

Jama'at Organizations of persons who travel to an area for the purposes of performing *daw'ah* among nonpracticing Muslims, or espousing a political view perceived to be in the (emergency) best interests of the *ummah*, or propagating Islam amongst non-Muslims.

Janaazah: The process of covering the dead body; the ritual washing of the deceased, and his or her burial and internment in accordance with Islamic tradition.

Jihad "Striving," "exertion." The struggle to be excellent in every endeavor a Muslim attempts or finds him/herself in; war in defense of Islam.

Jumah Congregational Islamic prayers performed on Fridays beginning after the sun passes its zenith.

Ka'aba The cube-shaped structure in the city of Mecca constructed by the Prophet Adam and later reconstructed by the Prophet Abraham and his son, around which Muslims perform the rituals of *hajj*, at least once in their lives.

Khutbah The Qur'anic reading and interpretation at the Friday congregation *al salat*.

Mahdi "Guide," "leader," who appears to restore justice to the land and begin a new world order.

Mahr The Arabic for "dowry," which the groom is required to give to his wife at the time of marriage.

Majlis as-Shura A council of Muslim leaders who consult with each other in community matters in the community's best interest.

Masha'allah Arabic for "May it please Allah."

Masjid The place of prostration. Where Muslims gather to perform prayer and other community rituals and observances.

Mecca The city in Arabia to which Muslim pilgrims travel in order to fulfill the fifth pillar of Islam.

Medina A city in Arabia located to the northeast of Mecca, formerly called Yathrib, to which Muhammad migrated in response to their leaders' invitation that he be Prophet and Ruler there.

Messiah: The anointed one; the anticipated King and deliverer of the Jews; also "one wiped clean," i.e., anointed (with oil) for a role.

Monotheism The belief or doctrine that there is only one god.

Moors A Muslim people of mixed Berber ancestry now living chiefly in Northern Africa, particularly Morocco.

Muhammad ibn Abdullah The last prophet in a line that includes Abraham, Moses, and Jesus.

Muslim One who submits oneself to the will of Allah as established in the Qur'an.

Nikkah The act of giving a woman in marriage. The contracted marital relationship of Muslim men and women.

Niyyah One's intention to do a thing whether in obedience or disobedience of Allah.

Pilgrimage Refers to the traveling of Muslims to Mecca in order to perform specific rites, at least once in their lives.

Polygyny The practice of having two or more wives at one time.

Qur'an "The Recitation," "the Guidance" from Allah to the Prophet Muhammad in fulfilment of Allah's promise/covenant with Prophet Abraham; the last revelation to come from Allah.

Qur'anic Under the influence of or being based in the Qur'an.

Ramadan The ninth month of the Islamic calendar in which Muslims fast from sunrise to sunset.

Retentions A phrase commonly used to communicate the collection of memories and artifacts that a people have of the culture from which they left, as related through literature, behaviors, and ritual.

Riba Usury, any profit from the sale or loan of goods, property, or cash money.

Rosicrucians An international fraternity of religious mysticism originating in the seventeenth and eighteenth centuries, devoted to the application of religious doctrine to modern life.

Salaam Becoming safe or secure, being at peace; part of the Islamic greeting "*As-Salaamu 'Alaikum*".

Salah Worship of Allah which Muslims perform five times daily in standing, bowing, prostrating, and kneeling postures, and with recitation aloud and silently, from the Qur'an.

Salat Formal Islamic prayer.

Sawm Self-restraint in the month of Ramadan, commonly translated as "fasting."

Shahadah The required profession of faith, a fundamental belief in Islam. ("There is no god except Allah and Muhammad is the messenger of Allah.") Announced by each person in order to be considered as Muslim.

Shariah "The way to the watering hole." Islamic law, which is based upon the Qur'an and the traditions of Muhammad ibn Abdullah.

Shi'a "Party," "faction." The party of 'Ali, who believed that 'Ali should have been the successor to Prophet Muhammad and the next leader of the Muslims.

Sufism The "mystical path" of Islam, derived from the Arabic *sufi*, a student of that path.

Sunnah The "way," "path," or body of traditions of the Prophet Muhammad.

Tajwid The science of recitation of the Qur'an.

Tasawwuf The Arabic term for Sufism, which is the "mystical path" of Islam.

Tauheed The unity of Alah. The concept which means that there is no deity except Allah.

Ummah The community of Muslim believers.

Wali A friend; relative, protector.

Worldview The way a person sees her/himself and everything other than her/himself in accordance with a discipline or philosophy.

X In The Nation of Islam the symbol has a double meaning: implying "ex," it signifies that believers are no longer who they were; and as "X ," it signifies an unknown quality or quantity.

Zakat The mandated contribution of 2.5 percent from one's earnings (of at least a specified value), computed at the end of the lunar year to help meet the financial needs of the *ummah.*

Notes

Introduction

1. For more information in this area of scholarship, see Allen Austin, *African Muslims in Antebellum America: A Sourcebook*; Clyde Ahmed Winters, "Roots and Islam in Slave America," *All-Ittihad* II (October-November, 1976), 18-20, and "A Survey of Islam and the African Diaspora," *Pan-African Journal* 8 (1975), 10-12.

Chapter 1 : The Early Communities

1. Historians of this community say that everywhere Noble Drew Ali visited he started a community.

2. The time of the establishment of the Moorish Science Temple was an historical era of redefinition of identity and reflection on the continuing oppression of black people, who were supposed to be accepted as American but in effect were still very much slaves.

3. See Peter Lamborn Wilson *Sacred Drift: Essays on the Margins of Islam* (San Francisco: City Lights Books, 1993), 16: "According to Drew Ali, blacks are "Asiatics," specifically Moors, that is, decendants

of the biblical Moabites through the Prophetess Ruth, later the inhabitants of Western Africa or Morocco. . . . Going back yet further, he believed his ancestors were Canaanites."

4. See Wilson J. Moses, *The Wings of Ethiopia: Studies in African American Life,* Ames: Iowa State University Press, 1990. Wilson examines the possibilities of Islamic retentions as the "African" retentions so often asserted.

5. See Wilson, *Sacred Drift* 17. Here Wilson asserts, "The hypothesis of a Moorish origin for at least some American blacks has been taken up by historians inspired by the *Golden Age of the Moor,* edited by Ivan Van Sertima, New Brunswick, N. J.: Transaction Publishers, 1993. . . . Soon after 1492 the Spanish were sending black slaves to the New World, some of whom are known to have been Moors or Moriscos. Some authors have even suggested that Moors and other Africans have reached the New World before Columbus. . . . .Whatever the case, clearly Moorish Moslems were among the first "discoverers of America."

6. This information on the Moorish Science Temple's history was provided by Muhammad al-Ahari, who has researched this community's history for at least a decade. Mr. Bektashi has recently finished writing a text on the Moorish Science Temple in all its stages of development, to be published soon.

7. Noble Drew Ali, *Moorish Literature* (no date or place of publicaton), 10.

8. There were several English translations and commentaries of the *Qur'an* in existence at this time. A. Ross produced an English translation of a French translation by Du Ryer in the mid-seventeenth century; George Sale's translation of a Latin version was published in 1734; Rev. J. M. Rodwell produced a chronological arrangement of the suras in 1851. According to Yusef Ali, the first Muslim translation was that of Dr. Muhammad 'Abdul Hakim Khan of Patiala in 1905. Whether any of these translations were available to African American Muslims at the turn of the twentieth century is still a question, and a further question arises when one pursues the understandings conceivable from one of the orientalist translations.

9. It has often been stated that members of this community were illiterate. Substantial evidence to the contrary is building as researchers look into the information used by this community. Noble Drew Ali chose some literature over others and some degree of literacy was necesary for the compilation of his *Circle Seven Koran,* the

pamphlet *The Koran Questions* used by the community, and the initiation of newspapers.

10. Noble Drew Ali *The Holy Koran of the Moorish Science Temple of America* (1927), P.3.

11. Wilson, *Sacred Drift, p.3*

12. One informant related that "on many occasions the City Hall would look at I.D. cards and acknowledge that we were not Negroes and permit us to write Moor in the space for race or ethnicity."

13. This information was given in a conversation with Sheik Danny Brown-El of the St. Louis temple on 29, October 1993.

14. The *Qur'an* clearly indicates three-times-daily prayer in three different places. The practice of five-times-daily prayer originates in the traditions of Prophet Muhammad ibn Abdullah. The Moorish Science Temple is not alone in this adherence, as Ismaili Muslims also pray three times daily.

15. It is interesting to note here that the information in the texts of the Moorish Science Temple share a great deal of similar teachings with the literature of the Druze of Syria. When asked, Mr. al-Ahari stated that this was not only possible but probable because of the number of Druze living in the immediate area. Druze are a community of people who call themselves "Islamic" but are not Muslim. For further information on their history, see Robert B. Betts *The Druze* (New Haven: Yale University Press, 1988); Abdallah Najjar, *The Druze*, trans. Fred I. Massey (American Druze Society, 1973). Many of the ideas in the Moorish Science literature are widespread among numerous Shiite groups throughout the Muslim world.

16. *Koran Questions for Moorish Americans*, 1.

17. Interviews with Ameenah Bey in 1988 and with Brown-El in 1993 substantiated this information.

18. The last *Moorish Science Monitor*, according to Peter Lamborn Wilson, appeared in 1966, but the journal was revived in 1986. It is the publication of the Moorish Orthodox Church of America which was "founded in the late 1950s by Europeans who (according to oral sources) had obtained Moorish Science Temple passports as 'Celts' or 'Persians'." (*Sacred Drift*, 49).

19. Wilson, *Sacred Drift,* 46.

20. For a detailed account of the Ahmadiyya Movement, see Yohanan Friedman, *Prophecy Continuous.* Berkeley, CA: University of California Press, 1989

21. *Bukhari* and *Muslim* are two of the recognized and accepted collections of the sayings and actions of Prophet Muhammad.

22. "Missionary" is a term used by the community for those members trained to teach the fundamentals of Islam and the history of the Ahmadi community.

23. The door to revelation and prophethood was not closed with the Prophet Muhammad. The coming Messiah literally has many of the same spiritual qualities of Jesus. Ahmadis believe that Islam and the Qur'an are the last religion and revealed scripture, and that Muhammad is the last law-bearing prophet. A prophet can come after him, but only as a Muslim and servant of Muhammad. For a complete discussion of this issue, see Mirza Bashir-ud-Din Mahmud Ahmad, *Introduction to the Study of the Holy Qur'an.* Surrey, United Kingdom: Islam International Publications, 1989.

24. See Arthur Fausets *Black Gods of the Metropolis* (Philadelphia: University of Pennsylvania Press, 1944), and R Laurence Moore *Religious Outsiders,* (New York: Oxford University Press, 1986)

25. Mirza Bashir-ud-Din Mahmud Ahmad. *Introduction to the Study of the Holy Qur'an,* 434.

26. It should be noted here that while some musicians did participate in the bebop movement, others (Yusef Lateef, for example) consciously did not play with bebop artists and took their music into developments that reflected their Islamic spirituality. In many ways these men expanded the Islamic influence in American culture in general. Their names were widely known and used for naming male children. The influence of these men on American music has not as of yet been thoroughly explored. Biographies and autobiographies focus on their experiences as musicians and make little mention of Islam.

27. This information on musicians was obtained in a conversation with Ahmadi historian and Islamic scholar, Oran Makin.

28. This information was gathered from letters written by Wali Akram complaining that African Americans were not appointed to positions

of leadership, and that was the reason that he and several other black men were severing their relationship with the community. His sons and grandsons have continued the legacy established in this community. As of this writing, this community is still vibrant and possibly even growing. Members are very warm and outgoing, providing a wealth of historical information.

29. Shaykh Dauod, who died in 1984, claimed that his mother was from Grenada and that his father was Moroccan. In his early adulthood he was an active jazz musician. The *Saudi News* (1960) quotes his as saying that he converted at least 30,000 AfricanAmericans to Islam prior to 1959.

30. "This was the first African American community to designate itself as "Sunni," In this context "Sunni" meant the Muslim world in general, rather than as in distinction from Shi'ite understandings of the Caliphate.

31. This information was revealed to me in a conversation with Dr. Sulayman Nyang about his interview with Khadijah Faisal, the Shakyh's wife in the 1980s.

32. *Sahabiyat* is the feminine plural (Arabic) word meaning "female group, grouped together, to work for common cause." *Sahabi'yat* 1, 4, 150.

33. The contents of this first edition are an assumption based on the contents of the second edition, which was published in 1965.

34. Members of the First Mosque of Cleveland assert that the First Mosque of Pittsburgh is an offshoot of the First Mosque of Cleveland. Given the wealth of evidence for the claim, I assume it to be true. Wali Akram, Imam of the First Mosque of Cleveland kept meticulous records of the members of the early community that date back to 1930. I am in the process of collecting these records, which list birth name, Muslim name, date of entry into the community, and date of death. Most of the people were at least forty years old when they became Muslim.

35. Most of the information on this community comes from two sources, Jameela A. Hakim, *History of the First Muslim Mosque of Pittsburgh, Pennsylvania* (no date or site of publication), and the archives of Farid Nu'man, senior researcher of the American Muslim Council.

36. Hakim, *History of the First Muslim Mosque of Pittsburgh.*

37. A conflicting claim arises here. The First Mosque of Pittsburgh claims to have issued a subcharter to Cleveland, while the records at the Cleveland Mosque claim that they gave the charter to Pittsburgh.

38. C. Eric Lincoln. *The Black Muslims in America* (New York: Beacon Press, 1961) 115

39. Benjamin Ringer, *"We the People" and Others* (New York: Routledge 1992 reprint), 178.

40. *Op. cit.* p. 179

41. Elijah Muhammad, *The Supreme Wisdom* (Newport News, Va.: The National Newport News and Commentator, 1957); 4.

42. *Ibid.*

43. "The Nation of Islam," *African Mirror,* Aug-Sept. 1979, p 45.

44. By 1972 there were fourteen University of Islam shcools in operation in the United States. Information researched by Eric Lincoln.

45. Lincoln, *The Black Muslims in America* 127-28 notes that the Nation of Islam had a series of one-time publications that researchers would find of interest. *The Messenger,* a magazine edited by Malcolm X; the *Islamic News,* a tabloid devoted to an historic Washington speech of Elijah Muhammad; *Salaam,* a pocket-sized magazine that featured Elijah Muhammad's first trip to Mecca and other appearances in Detroit and Chicago; and *Muhammad Speaks to the Blackman,* a "shallow publication playing on racial feeling. . . ."

46. Alex Haley, *The Autobiography of Malcolm X* (New York: Ballantine Books, 1964), 162-63.

47. Leadership in early African American Muslim communities parallesls that in Sufi Islam, where disciples are devoutly and often blindly obedient to the Sufi Master and his guidance.

Chapter 2 : Contemporary Communities

1. John L. Esposito, "Introduction, " in *Voices of Resurgent Islam,* ed. John L. Esposito, (New York: Oxford University Press, 1983), 5.

2. William L. Cleveland. *A History of the Modern Middle East* (San Francisco: Westview Press, 1994), 113.

3. See *The Turban for the Crown: The Islamic Revolution in Iran,* Sa'id Amir Arjomand, (New York: Oxford University Press 1989).

4. Yvonne Haddad, "Sayyid Qutb: Idelogue of Islamic Revival," *Voices of Resurgent Islam.*

5. Sayyid Qutb, *Milestones* (Cedar Rapids, Iowa: Unity Publishing Company, n.d.), 78.

6. *Ibid.* 118.

7. *Ibid.* 119.

8. *Ibid.* 130.

9. Charles J. Adams, "Mawdudi: and the Islamic State," in Esposito ed., *Voices of Resurgent Islam*, 101.

10. Abdul Ala Maududi, *Purdah and the Status of Women in Islam* 82. Translated and edited by Al-Ash'avi (Lahore, Pakistan: Islamic Publications Limited, 1972)

11. Sayid Qutb, *Milestones* (Cedar Rapids, Iowa: Unity Publishing Company, n.d.), 20

12. For more details on the civil rights movement, see: Taylor Branch *Parting the Waters* (New York: Simon and Schuster, 1988); David Garrow, *Bearing Cross* (New York: William Morrow, 1986); Aldon Morris, *The Origins of the Civil Rights Movement* (New York: Free Press, 1984); Juan Williams, *Eyes on the Prize: America's Civil Rights Years,* 195465 (New York: Penguin, 1988); Vincent Harding, *Hope and History,* (Maryknoll, N.Y.: Orbis Books, 1990).

13. Clayborne Carson, *In Struggle: SNCC and the Black Awakening of the 1960s* (Cambridge: Harvard University Press, 1981, 215.

14. *Ibid.* 216.

15. Stokely Carmichael and Charles V. Hamilton, *Black Power: The Politics of Libertation in America* (New York: Vintage Books, 1967, 40.

16. C. Eric Lincoln, *Race, Religion, and the Continuing American Dilemma*

1984 (New York: Hill and Wang), 91.

17. Although the list of African American musicians who chose Islam as a worldview at one time in their lives, were sympathizers, or who joined communities with some Islamic heritage is long, here is a short list of some of the more recognizable names given to me by Wali Muhammed of radio station 102 FM in Chicago: Phil Cohran, Jimmy Smith, John Coltrane, Yusef Lateef, Miles Davis, Rashaan Roland Kirk, Sarah Vaughn, Louis Armstrong, West Montgomery, Grover Washington, McCoy Tyner, Gene Ammons, Sonny Stitt, Betsy Smith, Billie Holiday, Carmen McRae, Quincy Jones, Ella Fitzgerald, Dexter Gordon, and Pharaoh Sanders.

18. Karl Evanzz, *The Judas Factor: The Plot to Kill Malcolm X* (New York: Thunder's Mouth Press, 1992), 114.

19. *Tablighi jama'at* originally referred to groups of Muslim men in India who travel around locally to "bring born Muslims back to Islam." This activity spread beyond the subcontinent and took on the task of traveling around the United States, especially in the 1970s and 1980s, teaching local Muslims and Islam.

20. Noble Drew Ali, *A Centennial Celebration: 1886-1986*, 26.

21. See *Ahmadiyyat in America.* Compiled by Mubasher Ahmad and Nasir A. Jamil under the supervision of Mirza Muzafar Ahmad. (Washington, D. C.: The Ahmadiyyah Movement), 1993. pg. 3.

22. A successor, a vicegerent, a deputy. The word is used in the Qur'an for Adam, as the vicegerent of the Almighty on earth. In Islam it is the title given to the successor of Muhammad, who is vested with absolute authority.

23. See Appendix for an example of *bai'at* in the Ahmadiyya Movement in Islam.

24. "Black Gods of the Inner City," *Gnosis*, Fall 1992.

25. Telephone conversation with Father Lord Lael Great Mind Allah, September 1993. This list was given orally in the conversation.

26. *Ibid.*

27. *Ibid.*

28. Taken from a community flyer.

29. According to Yvonne Haddad, this community has branches in Africa, the Carribean, Canada, England, Germany, Guyana, India, Saudi Arabia, Singapor, and Uruguay. See Haddad, *Mission to America*, 105.

30 *Ibid.*, 107.

31. As Sayyid Isa Al Haadi Al Mahdi. *The Ansaar Cult.* (Brooklyn, N.Y.: The Original Tents of Kedar, 1989), 109.

32. *Ibid.* 109

33. *Ibid.* 55

34. As Sayyid Isa Al Haadi Al Mahdi, *The Ansaar Cult*, 171.

35. *Ibid.*

36. "Statement," *The Islamic Party of North America: Ideological Outlook and Membership Form.* Printed with every handbook.

37. *Vision*, June/July edition, n.d.,3.

38. *Ibid.*

39. *Organization in Islam* (Washington, D.C.: The Islamic Party), 1972, 1.

40. *Al-Islam*, Spring 1972, 2.

41. *Ibid.*, 16.

42. *Ibid.*, 5.

43. *Ibid.*

44. From transcription of audio-visual tape of dinner conversation attended by M. Hamid in 1989 in Chicago.

45. *Ibid.*

46. Pledge printed on sheet with room for dates and signatures.

47. Recorded in *Muhammad Speaks*, 21 March 1975.

48. See Clifton Marsh, *The World Community of Islam in the West: From Black Muslim to Muslim* (1931-1977) (Metuchen, N.J.: Scarecrow Press, 1984).

49. See Appendix for Actual Facts.

50. W. D. Muhammad. *Lectures of Emam Muhammad,* (Chicago: W. D Muhammad Publications, Inc., 1978), iv.

51. *Ibid.*, viii.

52. Emam Wallace D. Muhammad, *Lectures of Emam Muhammad* Chicago: W. D. Muhammad Publications, Inc., 1978, v.

53. Ibid.. 3. For detailed information on this era in the community's development, see Lawrence Mamiya, "From Black Muslim to Bilalian: the Evolution of a Movement," *Journal for the Scientific Study of Religion* 21, June 1982, 138–52; James Tinney, "Bilalian Muslims," *Christian Theology* 20, 12 March 1976, 51–52.

54. See *World Muslim News,* 1 January, 1982.

55. *Final Call,* November 1984.

56. *Final Call,* 31 October 1990.

57. *Final Call,* 30 June 1993.

58. Minister Farrakhan has recently reopened grocery stores and restaurants in Chicago.

59. *Final Call,* 15 March 1993.

60. *Muhammad Speaks Continues,* April 1993.

61. Imam Jamil Al-Amin, *Revolution by the Book* (Beltsville, Maryland: Writers' Inc. International, 1993), x.

62. *Ibid.*, xvi.

63. *Ibid.*, xvii.

64. *Ibid.*, 10.

65. *Ibid.*, 30.

66. *Ibid.*, 43.

67. *Ibid.*, 62

68. *Ibid.*, 68.

69. *Ibid.*, 121. *Qur'an* 4:75.

70. The discussion of sufism is far broader than can be attempted in this text. We only offer the briefest of introductions and refer the reader to several introductory texts such as: *Islamic Spirituality*. edited by Seyyed H. Nasr. vol 1. New York: Crossroad, 1987.

71. Abu Bakr Siraj Ed-Din, "The Nature and Origin of Sufism," in *Islamic Spirituality*. ed. by Seyyed H. Nasr. (New York: Crossroad, 1987), 233.

72. Saadia Khawar Khan Chishti. "Female Sprituality in Islam," in *Islamic Spirituality: Foundations*. edited by Seyyed Hossein Nasr. (New Yorkl: Crossroad, 1987), 199, 200.

73. Interview with Rashid Hassan in November, 1993.

74. Interview with Shakyh Ahmad Tijani in Chicago in November, 1993.

Chapter 3 : The Family Structure and Domestic Life

1. These advertisements were taken from *Islamic Horizons*, Spring 1992, and July/August 1989.

2. E.W. Lane, *Arabic-English Lexicon*, Vol. 2 (London: Williams and Norgate, 1877) 3060.

3. Recorded conversation on issue of polygyny with several women at Women's Conference in Chicago August, 1993.

4. For an extremely informative examination of human geography, see Benno Werlen, *Society, Action and Space*, (New York; Routledge, 1993).

5. Perhaps this change was a product of both foreign travel and the meeting of more African Muslims in the general community.

6. *Parents' Manual. A Guide for Muslim Parents Living in North America*, prepared by The Woman's Committee, The Muslim Students'

Association of the United States & Canada, World Community of Islam in the West, 1976, 3.

7. There are several Muslim publishing houses that have made educational materials for children their priority. One such house is Iqra located in Chicago.

8. Muhammad Abdullah al-Ahari Bektashi, "Noble Drew Ali, Moorish Science, and American Islamic Nationalism." Prepared for Vassar College, 1993.

9. For more detailed information on funerals and burial rites, there are a few exemplary general introduction to Islam texts, such as Frederick Denny, *An Introduction to Islam,* 2nd edition, New York: Macmillan, 1994; Thomas Lippman, *Understanding Islam,* New York: Mentor, 1990; Suzanne Haneef, *What Everyone Should Know About Muslims,* Chicago: Kazi Publications, 1973.

10. Janaaza Burial Program Brochure, Janaaza Planning Program, 1809 E. 71st, - Suite G, Chicago, Ill 60649

Chapter 4 : Social Issues and Challenges

1. Kamal Ali. "Islamic Education in the United States: An Overview of Issues, Problems and Possible Approaches," *The American Journal of Islamic Social Sciences,* 1984, 127–32.

2. Ali, "Islamic Education,", 129.

3. Mohammad Hashim Kamali, *Principles of Islamic Jurisprudence,* Cambridge: Islamic Texts Society, 1991, 7.

4. *Ibid.*

5. U.S.C.A. Const. Amend. 1

6. As examples, see *Yusuf Lateef Na'im Salahuddin v. Norman A. Carson, et al.,* Civ. A. No. 81-0224-R, United States District Court, E.D. Virginia, Richmond Division, 24 Sept, 1981; *Masjid Muhammad D.c.c. v. Keve,* 479 F. Supp. 1311 (D. Del. 1979) Civ. A. No. 77-221, United States District Court, Delaware, 22 Oct, 1979.

7. The Rights of Prisoners, *American Civil Civil liberties Union Handbook,* ed. Edward I. Koren and Alvin J. Bronstein, (Carbondale, Southern Illinois University Press), 1988, 49.

8. *Ibid.*, 49

9. *Ibid.*, 50.

10. Federick Thaufeer al-Deen, "African American Muslims in Prisons," unpublished, 1993.

11. Monzer, Kahf, *The Islamic Economy* (Plainfield: The MuslimStudents' Association of the United States and Canada, 1978)

12. *Ibid.*

13. Cited in Yvonne Haddad, *The Muslims of America, The Muslims of America.* ed by Yvonne Y. Haddad (New York: Oxford University Press, 1991), 111

Chapter 5 : Women in Islam

1. Sachiko Murata, *The Tao of Islam: A Source Book on Gender Relationships in Islamic Thought,* (New York: State University of New York Press, 1992), 1.

2. Wiebeke Walther, *Women in Islam from Medieval to Modern Times* (New York: Markus Weiner Publishing, Inc., 1993), 3.

3. Leila Ahmed, *Women and Gender in Islam,* (New Haven, Connecticut: Yale University Press, 1992), 149.

4. *Ibid.*, 151-52.

5. Fatima Mernissi, *The Veil and the Male Elite,* trans. Mary Jo Lakeland (New York: Addison-Wesley Publishing Company, Inc., 1991), 85. The remainder of this quote says ". . . but between two men." I assume this is an error in translation, because the ayah clearly is speaking about a curtain between visitors and the Prophet's wives.

6. *Ibid.*, 97.

7. *Ibid.*

8. Afzular Rahman, *Role of Muslim Women in Society* (London: Seerah Foundation, 1986) 1.

9. *Ibid..*, 2.

10. Hasa Al-Turabi. *Women in Muslim Society and Islam* (London: Milestone, 1973).

11. Rashid al-Ghanushi, *Al-Mara a-Muslim fi Tunis Bain Tawjeehat al-Qur'an was Wagi al-Mujtama al-Tunisi* (*The Muslim Women of Tunisia between the Directives of Qur'an and the Reality of the Tunisia Society*) (Kuwait: Dar al-Qalam , 1988). Some other recent texts that explore issues around women include: Abdul-Halim Abu Shaqa, *Tahreer al-Mara fi Asr al-Risala* (*The Liberation of Women in the Era of Revelation: A Comprehensive Study of Qur'an, Sahih Burkari, and Sahih Muslim Texts*)(Kuwait: Dar al-Kuwait, 1990); al-Turabi, *Al-Mara Bin Taa'lim al-Sharia's was Takalid al-Mujtama* (*Women between the teaching of Sharia and the Customs of Society*) (Sudan.)

12. Amina Wadud-Mushin, *Woman and the Qur'an* (Kuala Lumpur, Malaysia: Penerbit Fajar Bakit Sdn. Bhd., 1992), 8.

13. *Ibid.*, 15.

14. *Ibid.*, 29.

15. Ahmed, *Women and Gender in Islam* 4. I also note that there is no Eve in the *Qur'an* .

16. *Ibid.*, 5.

17. Hasan Al-Turabi

18. Hasan Al-Turabi.

19. bell hooks, *Talking Back* (Boston: South End Press, 1989), 6.

20. *Ibid.*, 79.

21. Ahmed, *Women and Gender in Islam*, 238.

22. Ibid., 239.

23. From *Final Call*, 10 May 1993.

24. From *Muhammad Speaks Continues,* December 1992.

25. Ayesha Mustafa, editor, *Muslim Journal,* 24 July 1993, 20.

26. Mildred El-Amin, *Family Roots,* (Chicago: International Ummah Foundation), 1991, 29.

Conclusion

1. Toshihiko Izutsu, *Ethico-Religious Concepts in the Qur'an,* (Montreal: McGill University Press), 1966, 45.

2. Benjamin Ringer. *"We The People" and Others,* (New York: Routledge, 1992), 105.